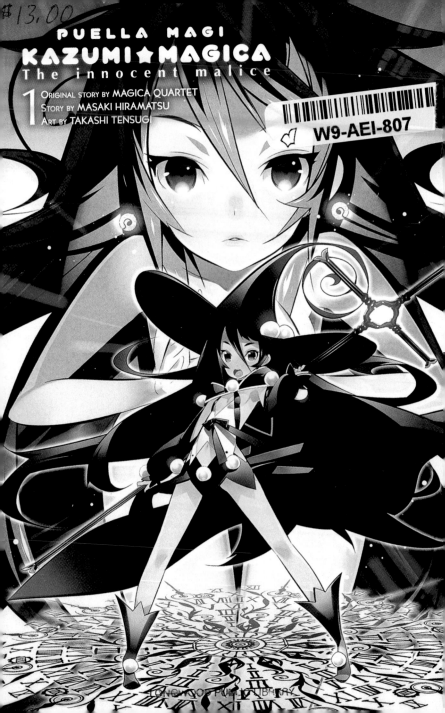

PUELLA MAGI
KAZUMI ★ MAGICA
The innocent malice

1 ORIGINAL STORY BY MAGICA QUARTET
STORY BY MASAKI HIRAMATSU
ART BY TAKASHI TENSUGI

1

PUELLA MAGI KAZUMI MAGICA
The innocent malice

Original story by Magica Quartet / Story by Masaki Hiramatsu / Art by Takashi Tensugi

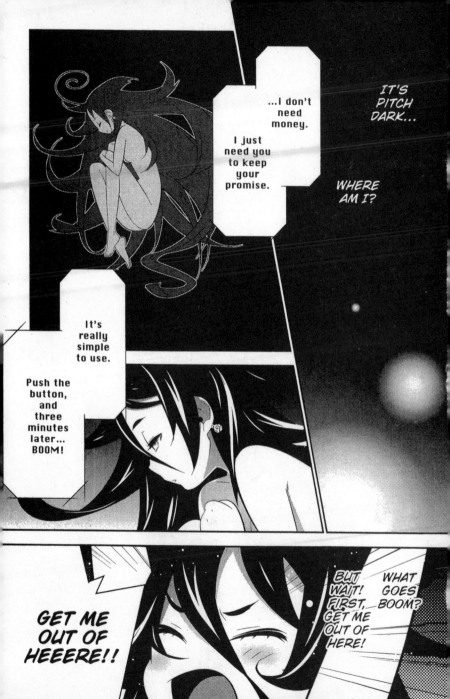

CHAPTER 1: SPOTABADDYNOFF

SO THE KIDNAPPER WHO SHUT ME IN A BOX...

...WAS YOUUUU!!

NOOO! LEMME GO!

GASHI (GRAB)

...

KAAAA
(BLUUUSH)

?

...

GUUUUUU
(GURRRGLE)

SO,
ONII-
SAN...

...YOU WERE GIVEN A TRUNK WITH A BOMB INSIDE...

...THAT WAS MEANT TO BE USED TO BLOW UP A SHOPPING CENTER.

BUT YOU'RE SAYING...

...THAT I WAS IN THE BOX INSTEAD?

...

KOKUN (NOD)

SO YOU DON'T WANT ME DEAD, AND THIS FOOD ISN'T POISONED?

...

KACHA (CLINK)

KACHA

MM! MMM! HUH? THIS IS REALLY GOOD!

NO, THIS IS GREAT!

WELL, THEN!

I'LL JUST DIG IN!!

WHERE DO YOU COOK? I WANT TO GO EAT THERE!

ONII-SAN, YOU MUST BE A PRO, HUH? THIS TASTES TOO GOOD!

KACHA

THANKS FOR THE FOOD!

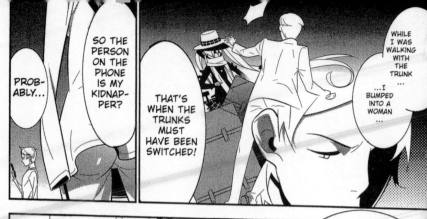

WHILE I WAS WALKING WITH THE TRUNK ...

...I BUMPED INTO A WOMAN...

SO THE PERSON ON THE PHONE IS MY KIDNAPPER?

PROBABLY...

THAT'S WHEN THE TRUNKS MUST HAVE BEEN SWITCHED!

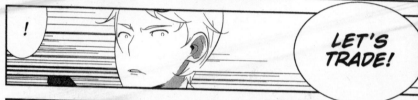

!

LET'S TRADE!

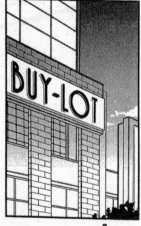

BUY-LOT

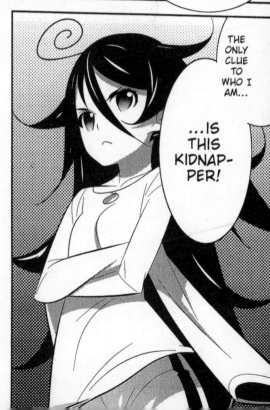

THE ONLY CLUE TO WHO I AM...

...IS THIS KIDNAPPER!

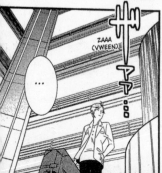

ZAAA (VWEEN)

...

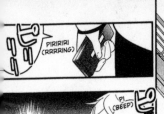

PIRIRIRI
(RRRRING)

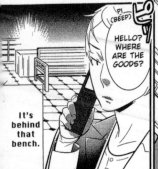

PI
(BEEP)

HELLO? WHERE ARE THE GOODS?

It's behind that bench.

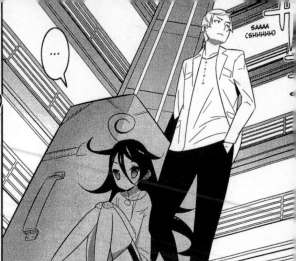

...

SAAAA
(SHHHHH)

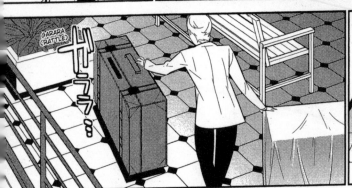

GARARA
(RATTLE)

...

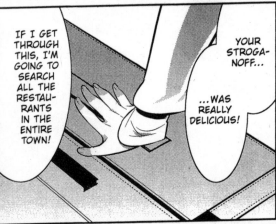

IF I GET THROUGH THIS, I'M GOING TO SEARCH ALL THE RESTAURANTS IN THE ENTIRE TOWN!

YOUR STROGANOFF...

...WAS REALLY DELICIOUS!

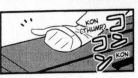

KON
(THUMP)

KON

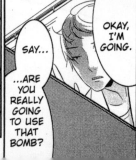

SAY...

...ARE YOU REALLY GOING TO USE THAT BOMB?

OKAY, I'M GOING.

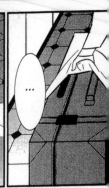

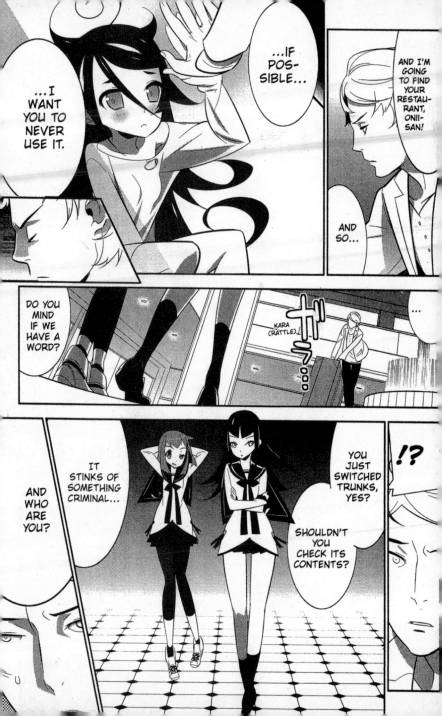

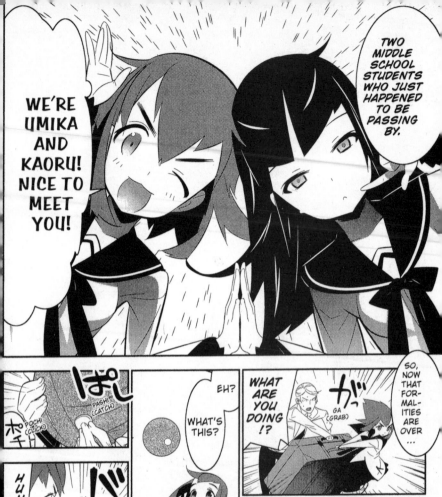

TWO MIDDLE SCHOOL STUDENTS WHO JUST HAPPENED TO BE PASSING BY.

WE'RE UMIKA AND KAORU! NICE TO MEET YOU!

PASHI (CATCH)

POCHI (CATCH)

EH?

WHAT'S THIS?

WHAT ARE YOU DOING!?

GA (GRAB)

SO, NOW THAT FORMALITIES ARE OVER...

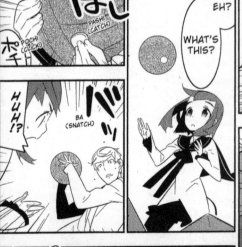

HUH!?

BA (SNATCH)

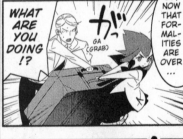

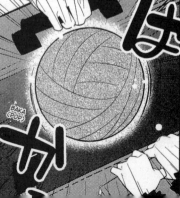

PI (PEEP)

0:00

BAKA (POP)

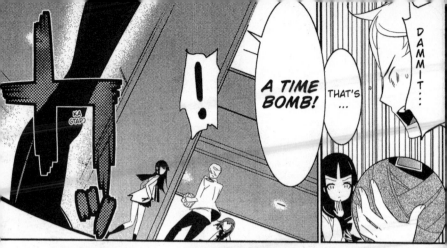

DAMMIT...

A TIME BOMB!

THAT'S...

KA (TAP)

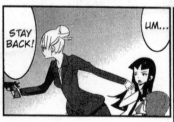

STAY BACK!

UM...

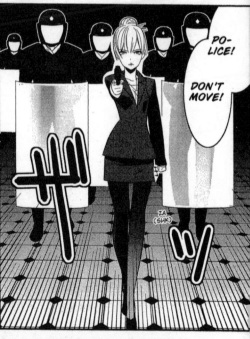

PO-LICE!

DON'T MOVE!

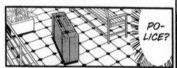

PO-LICE?

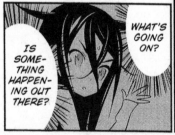

IS SOME-THING HAPPEN-ING OUT THERE?

WHAT'S GOING ON?

ZA (SHK)

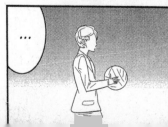

...

YOU'RE SOU-ICHIROU TACHI-BANA, COR-RECT?

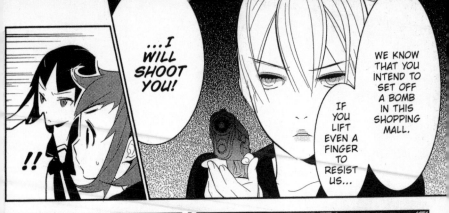

...I WILL SHOOT YOU!

WE KNOW THAT YOU INTEND TO SET OFF A BOMB IN THIS SHOPPING MALL.

IF YOU LIFT EVEN A FINGER TO RESIST US...

!!

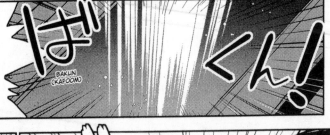

WAIT RIGHT THERE!!

バ (BAKUN) (KAFOOM)

くん!

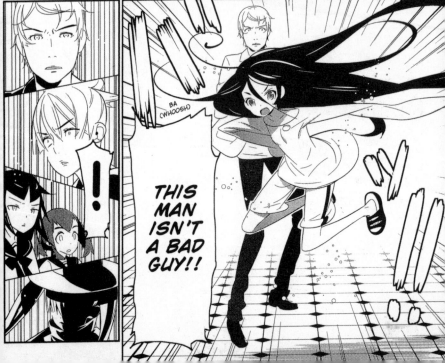

BA (WHOOSH)

!

THIS MAN ISN'T A BAD GUY!!

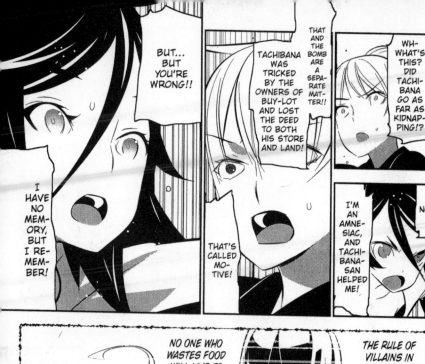

BUT... BUT YOU'RE WRONG!!

TACHIBANA WAS TRICKED BY THE OWNERS OF BUY-LOT AND LOST THE DEED TO BOTH HIS STORE AND LAND!

THAT AND THE BOMB ARE A SEPARATE MATTER!!

WH-WHAT'S THIS? DID TACHIBANA GO AS FAR AS KIDNAPPING!?

I HAVE NO MEMORY, BUT I REMEMBER!

THAT'S CALLED MOTIVE!

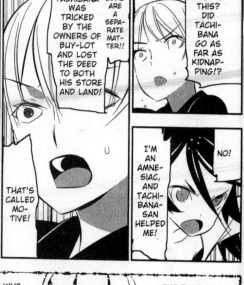

NO!

I'M AN AMNESIAC, AND TACHIBANA-SAN HELPED ME!

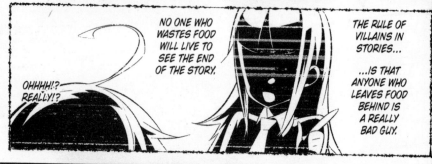

OHHHH!? REALLY!?

NO ONE WHO WASTES FOOD WILL LIVE TO SEE THE END OF THE STORY.

THE RULE OF VILLAINS IN STORIES...

...IS THAT ANYONE WHO LEAVES FOOD BEHIND IS A REALLY BAD GUY.

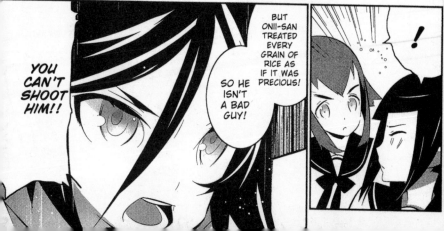

YOU CAN'T SHOOT HIM!!

BUT ONII-SAN TREATED EVERY GRAIN OF RICE AS IF IT WAS PRECIOUS!

SO HE ISN'T A BAD GUY!

!

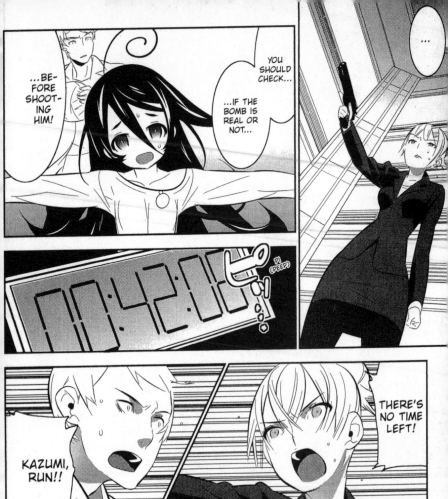

...BE-FORE SHOOT-ING HIM!

YOU SHOULD CHECK...

...IF THE BOMB IS REAL OR NOT...

...

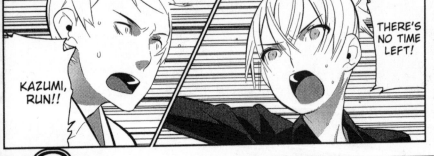

THERE'S NO TIME LEFT!

KAZUMI, RUN!!

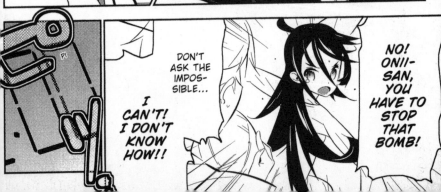

PI

DON'T ASK THE IMPOS-SIBLE...

I CAN'T! I DON'T KNOW HOW!!

NO! ONII-SAN, YOU HAVE TO STOP THAT BOMB!

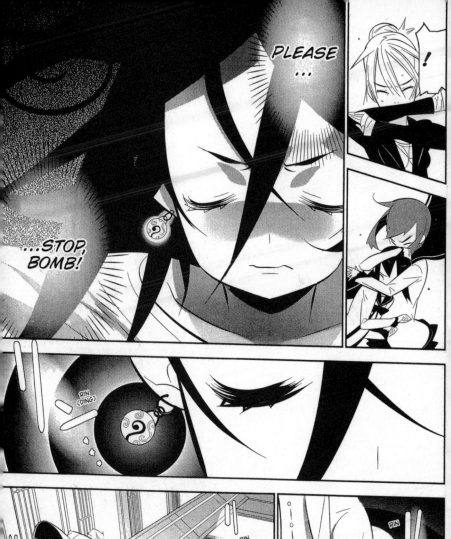

PLEASE
...

!

...STOP,
BOMB!

RIN
(DING)

RIN

RIN

RIN

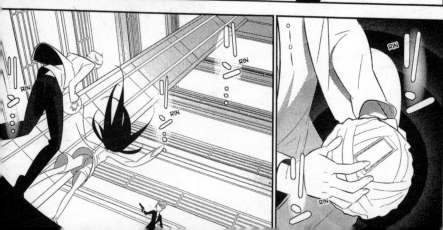

RIN

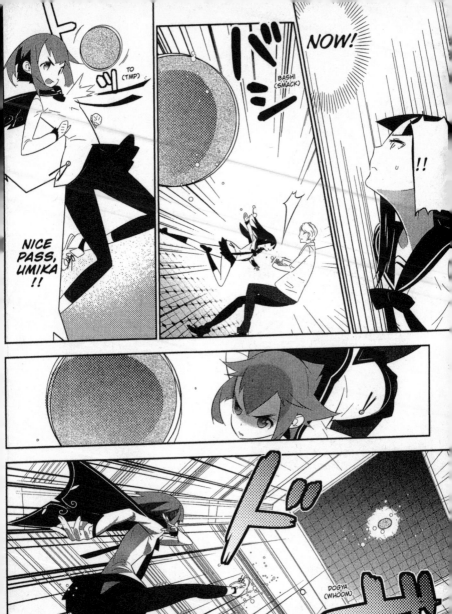
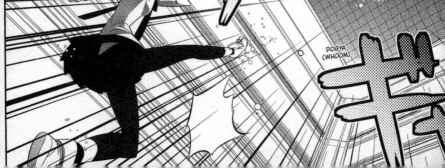

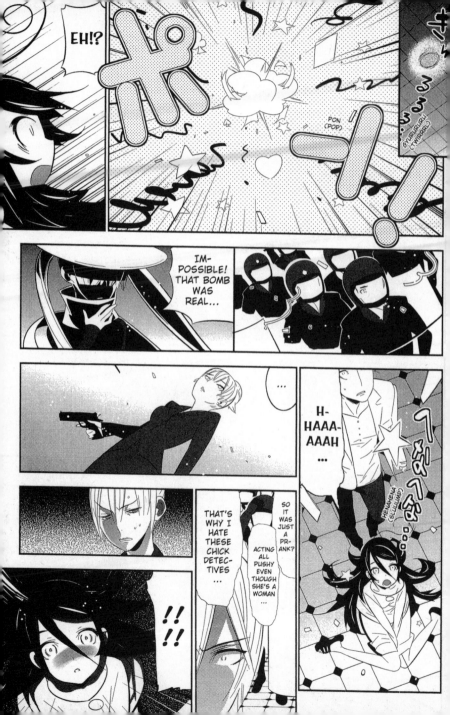

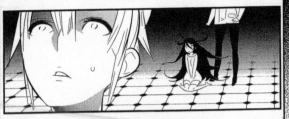

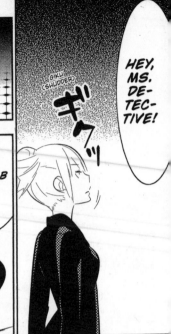

HEY, MS. DE-TEC-TIVE!

GIKU (SHUDDER)

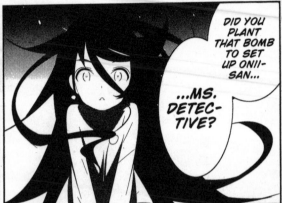

DID YOU PLANT THAT BOMB TO SET UP ONII-SAN...

...MS. DETEC-TIVE?

WHO...

...WHO DO YOU THINK YOU ARE?

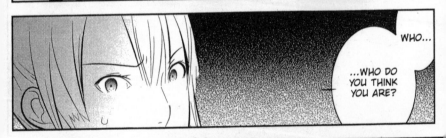

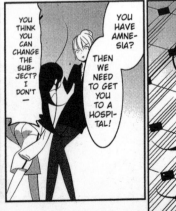

YOU THINK YOU CAN CHANGE THE SUBJECT? I DON'T —

YOU HAVE AMNE-SIA? THEN WE NEED TO GET YOU TO A HOSPI-TAL!

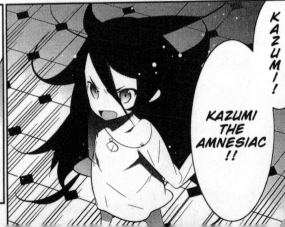

KAZUMI!

KAZUMI THE AMNESIAC !!

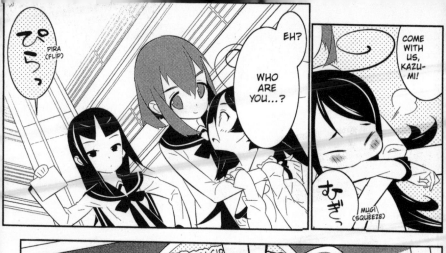

EH?

WHO ARE YOU...?

PIRA (FLIP)

COME WITH US, KAZU-MI!

MUGI (SQUEEZE)

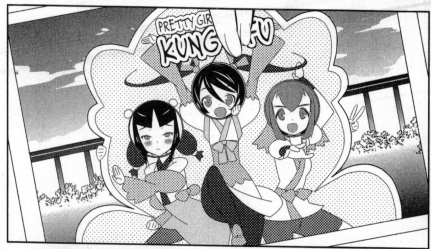

PRETTY GIRL KUNG FU

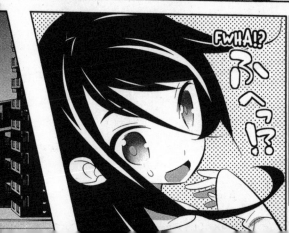

FWHA!?

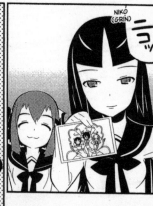

NIKO (GRIN)

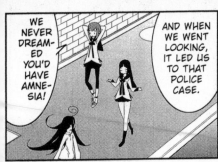

WE NEVER DREAM-ED YOU'D HAVE AMNESIA!

AND WHEN WE WENT LOOKING, IT LED US TO THAT POLICE CASE.

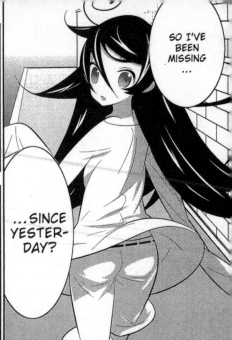

SO I'VE BEEN MISSING...

...SINCE YESTER-DAY?

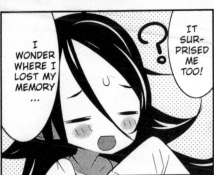

I WONDER WHERE I LOST MY MEMORY...

IT SURPRISED ME TOO!

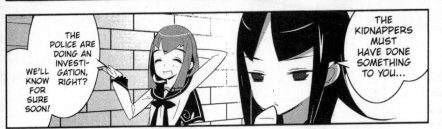

THE POLICE ARE DOING AN INVESTIGATION, RIGHT?

WE'LL KNOW FOR SURE SOON!

THE KIDNAPPERS MUST HAVE DONE SOMETHING TO YOU...

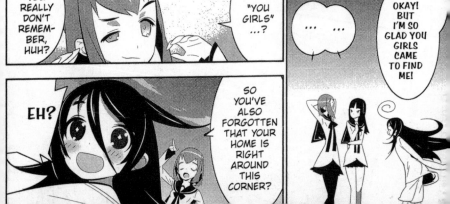

YOU REALLY DON'T REMEMBER, HUH?

"YOU GIRLS"...?

...   ...

OKAY! BUT I'M SO GLAD YOU GIRLS CAME TO FIND ME!

EH?

SO YOU'VE ALSO FORGOTTEN THAT YOUR HOME IS RIGHT AROUND THIS CORNER?

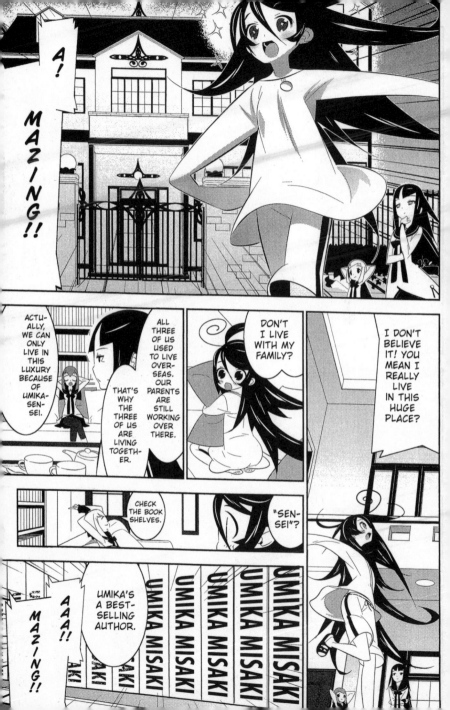

A! MAZING!!

ACTUALLY, WE CAN ONLY LIVE IN THIS LUXURY BECAUSE OF UMIKA-SENSEI.

THAT'S WHY THE THREE OF US ARE LIVING TOGETHER.

ALL THREE OF US USED TO LIVE OVERSEAS. OUR PARENTS ARE STILL WORKING OVER THERE.

DON'T I LIVE WITH MY FAMILY?

I DON'T BELIEVE IT! YOU MEAN I REALLY LIVE IN THIS HUGE PLACE?

CHECK THE BOOK SHELVES.

"SEN-SEI"?

UMIKA'S A BEST-SELLING AUTHOR.

A A A !! MAZING!!

UMIKA MISAKI

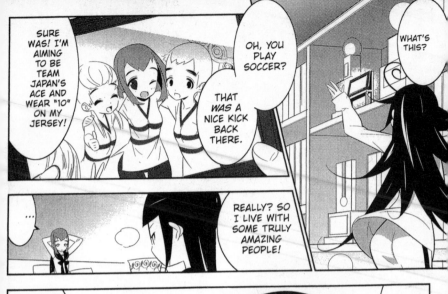

SURE WAS! I'M AIMING TO BE TEAM JAPAN'S ACE AND WEAR "10" ON MY JERSEY!

OH, YOU PLAY SOCCER?

THAT WAS A NICE KICK BACK THERE.

WHAT'S THIS?

...

REALLY? SO I LIVE WITH SOME TRULY AMAZING PEOPLE!

CAN I!?

WOULD YOU LIKE TO SEE YOUR ROOM?

YOU MIGHT RECALL SOMETHING.

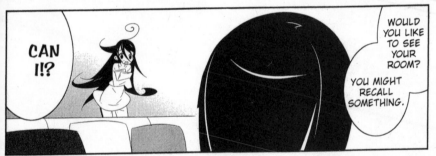

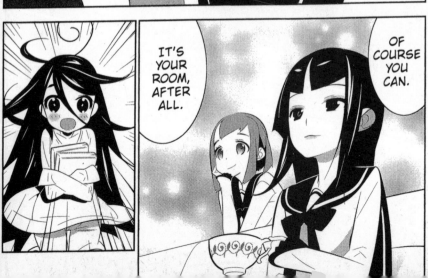

IT'S YOUR ROOM, AFTER ALL.

OF COURSE YOU CAN.

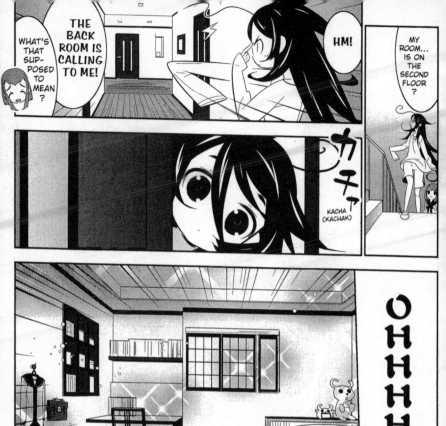

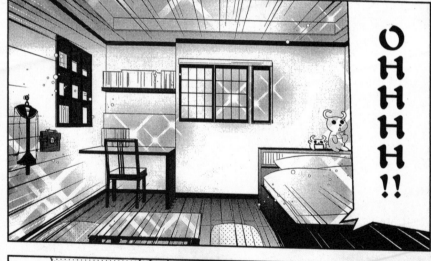

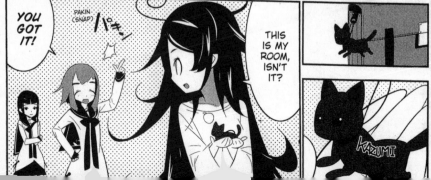

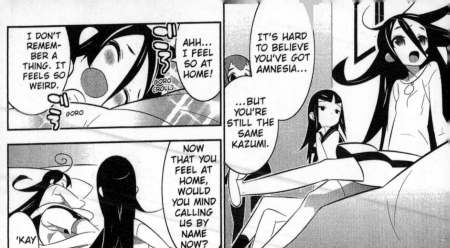

I DON'T REMEMBER A THING. IT FEELS SO WEIRD.

GORO (ROLL)

GORO

AHH... I FEEL SO AT HOME!

IT'S HARD TO BELIEVE YOU'VE GOT AMNESIA...

...BUT YOU'RE STILL THE SAME KAZUMI.

NOW THAT YOU FEEL AT HOME, WOULD YOU MIND CALLING US BY NAME NOW?

'KAY...

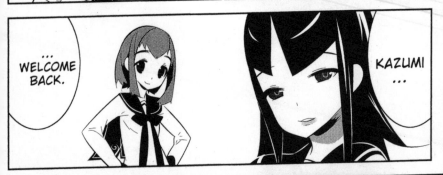

...WELCOME BACK.

KAZUMI...

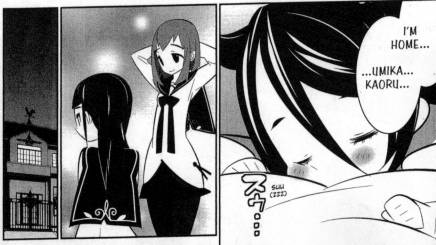

I'M HOME...

...UMIKA... KAORU...

SUU (ZZZ)

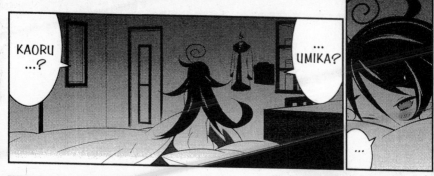

KAORU...?

...UMIKA?

...

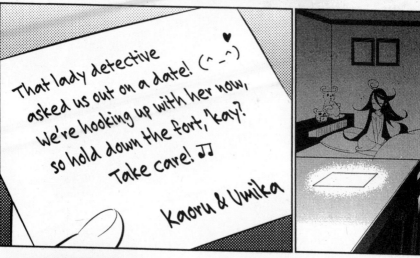

That lady detective asked us out on a date! (^_^)♥ We're hooking up with her now, so hold down the fort, 'kay? Take care! ♪♪

Kaoru & Umika

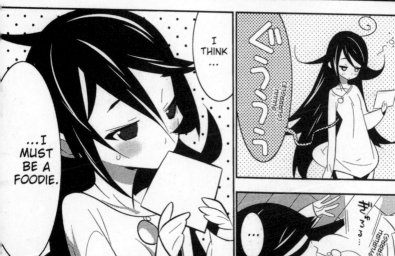

I THINK...

....

(GURGGLE)

...I MUST BE A FOODIE.

...

(GRRRG)

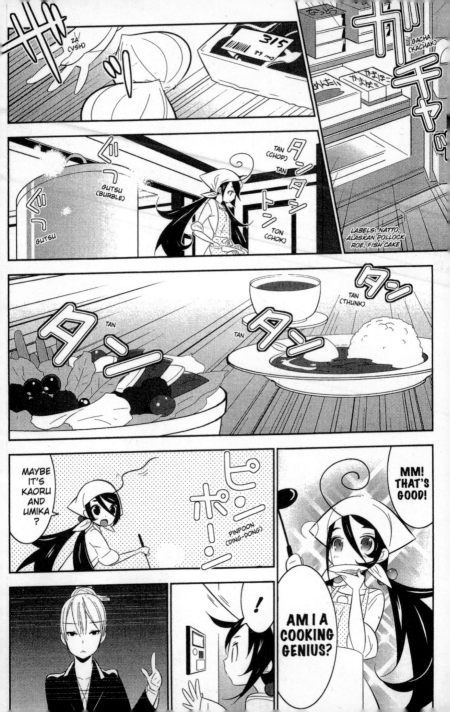

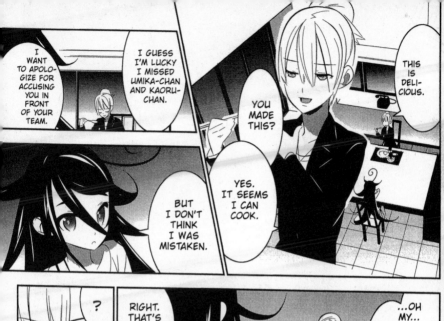

I WANT TO APOLO-GIZE FOR ACCUSING YOU IN FRONT OF YOUR TEAM.

I GUESS I'M LUCKY I MISSED UMIKA-CHAN AND KAORU-CHAN.

THIS IS DELI-CIOUS.

YOU MADE THIS?

BUT I DON'T THINK I WAS MISTAKEN.

YES. IT SEEMS I CAN COOK.

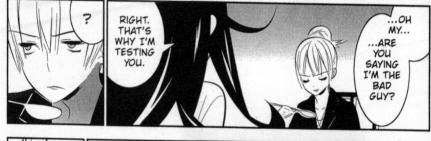

?

RIGHT. THAT'S WHY I'M TESTING YOU.

...OH MY...

...ARE YOU SAYING I'M THE BAD GUY?

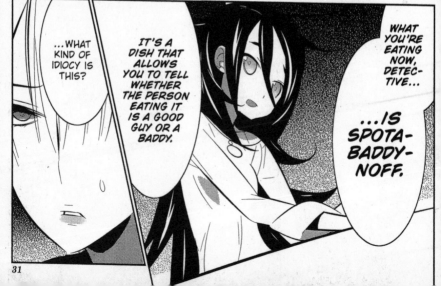

...WHAT KIND OF IDIOCY IS THIS?

IT'S A DISH THAT ALLOWS YOU TO TELL WHETHER THE PERSON EATING IT IS A GOOD GUY OR A BADDY.

WHAT YOU'RE EATING NOW, DETEC-TIVE...

...IS SPOTA-BADDY-NOFF.

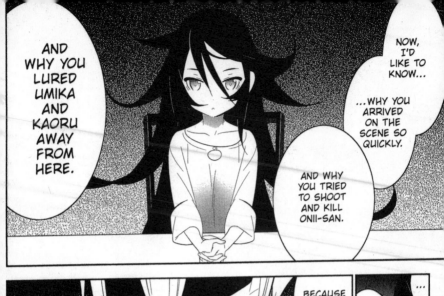

NOW, I'D LIKE TO KNOW...

...WHY YOU ARRIVED ON THE SCENE SO QUICKLY.

AND WHY YOU LURED UMIKA AND KAORU AWAY FROM HERE.

AND WHY YOU TRIED TO SHOOT AND KILL ONII-SAN.

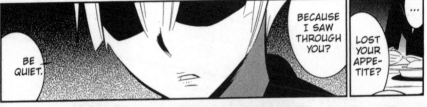

...

LOST YOUR APPETITE?

BECAUSE I SAW THROUGH YOU?

BE QUIET.

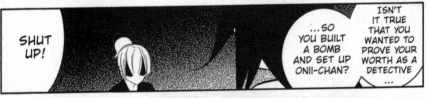

ISN'T IT TRUE THAT YOU WANTED TO PROVE YOUR WORTH AS A DETECTIVE...

...SO YOU BUILT A BOMB AND SET UP ONII-CHAN?

SHUT UP!

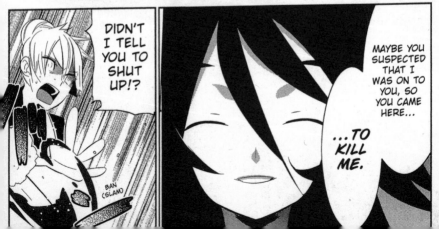

DIDN'T I TELL YOU TO SHUT UP!?

BAN (SLAM)

MAYBE YOU SUSPECTED THAT I WAS ON TO YOU, SO YOU CAME HERE...

...TO KILL ME.

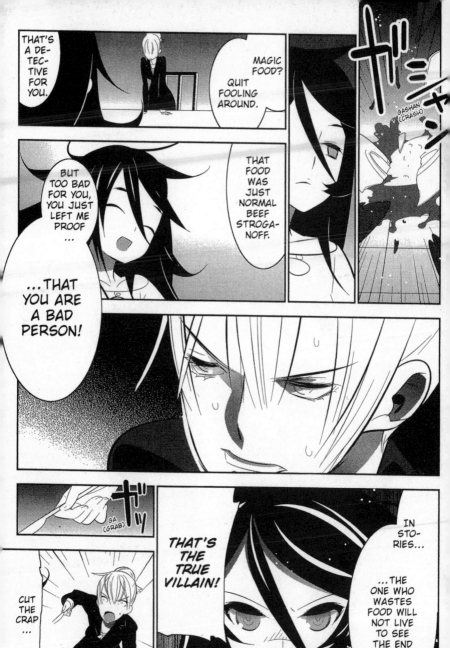

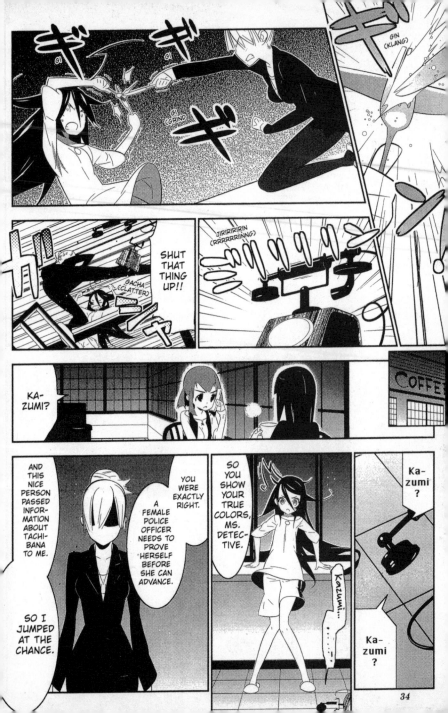

GI

GI

GI (GRIND)

GIN (KLANG)

SHUT THAT THING UP!!

GACHA (CLATTER)

JIRIRIRIRIN (RRRRRRIIIING)

KA-ZUMI?

COFFE

AND THIS NICE PERSON PASSED INFORMATION ABOUT TACHI-BANA TO ME.

YOU WERE EXACTLY RIGHT.

A FEMALE POLICE OFFICER NEEDS TO PROVE HERSELF BEFORE SHE CAN ADVANCE.

SO YOU SHOW YOUR TRUE COLORS, MS. DETEC-TIVE.

Ka-zumi?

Kazumi....

SO I JUMPED AT THE CHANCE.

Ka-zumi?

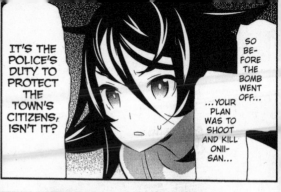

I RECEIVED MORE THAN INFORMATION FROM THAT INFORMANT. I GOT POWER TOO!

IT'S THE POLICE'S DUTY TO PROTECT THE TOWN'S CITIZENS, ISN'T IT?

SO BEFORE THE BOMB WENT OFF...

...YOUR PLAN WAS TO SHOOT AND KILL ONII-SAN...

IT'S A POWER THAT WILL ALLOW ME TO MURDER A PERSON LEAVING ABSOLUTELY NO EVIDENCE BEHIND.

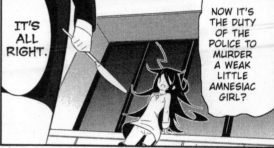

IT'S ALL RIGHT.

NOW IT'S THE DUTY OF THE POLICE TO MURDER A WEAK LITTLE AMNESIAC GIRL?

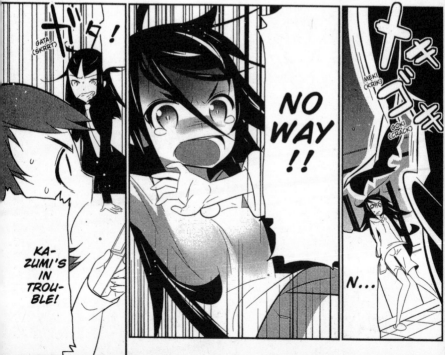

GATA!! (SKRRT)

NO WAY!!

KAZUMI'S IN TROUBLE!

MEKI (KRIK)

GOKI (CRACK)

N...

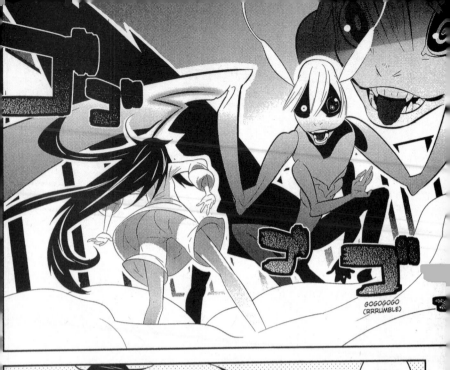

GOGOGOGO
(RRRUMBLE)

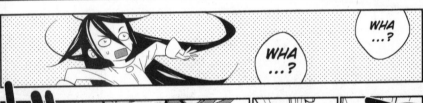

WHA
...?

WHA
...?

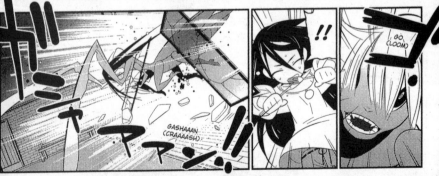

!!

GO
(LOOM)

GASHAAAN
(CRAAAASH)

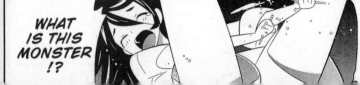

WHAT
IS THIS
MONSTER
!?

WHAT'S
GOING
ON!?

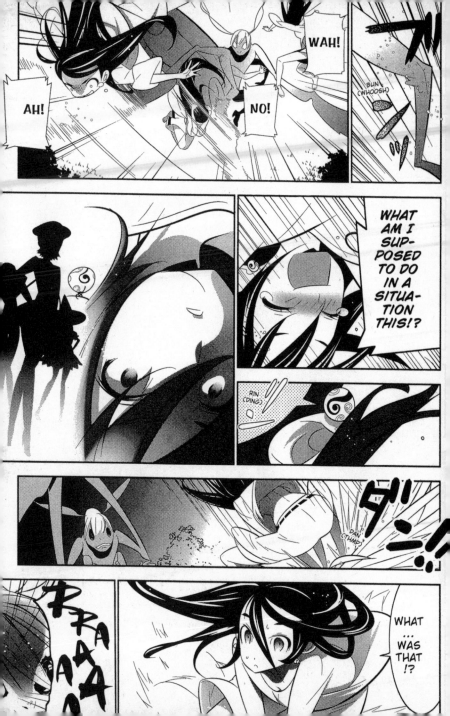

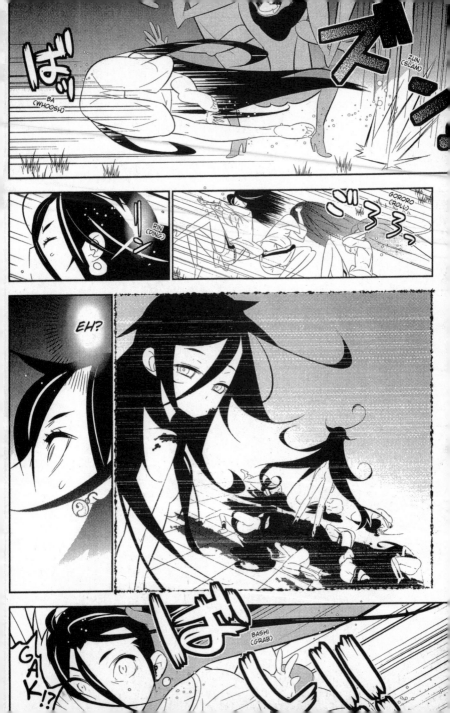

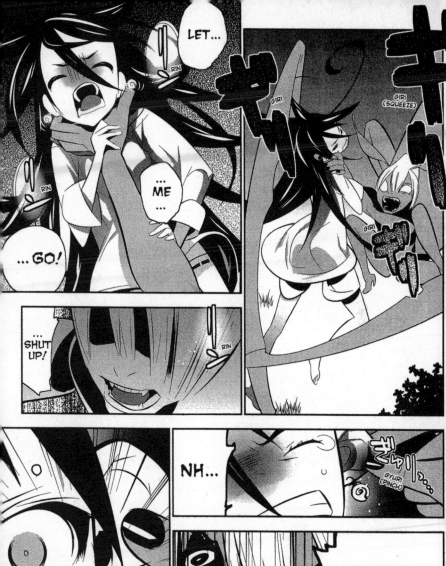
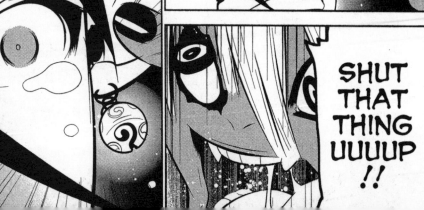

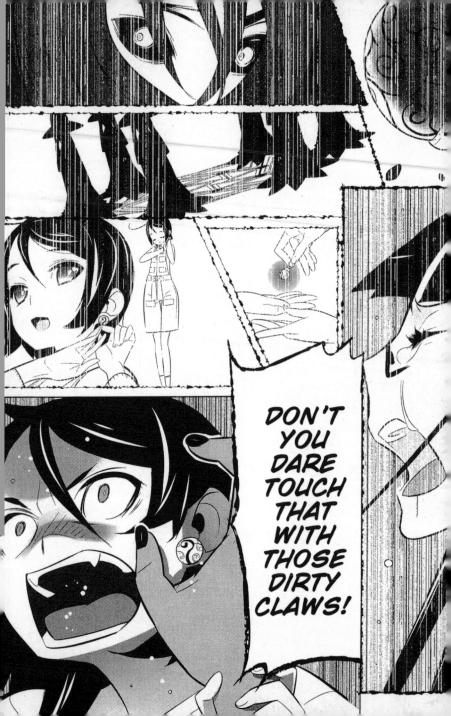

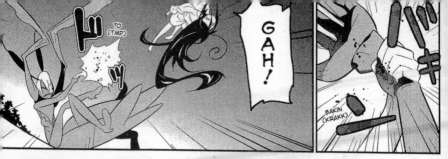

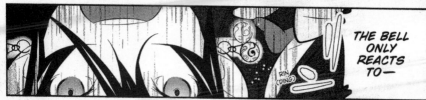

THE BELL
ONLY
REACTS
TO—

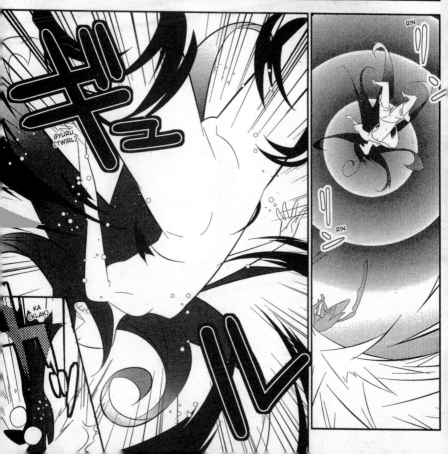

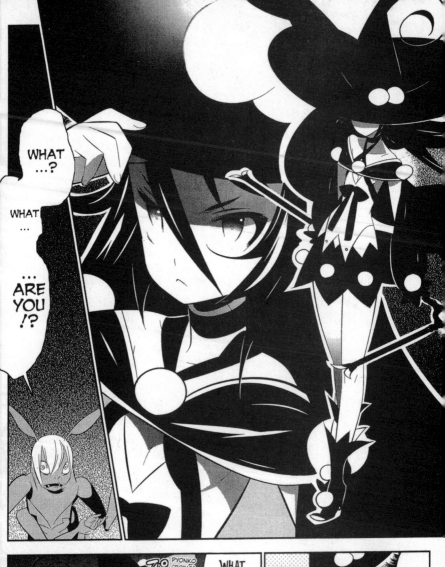

WHAT...?

WHAT...

...ARE YOU!?

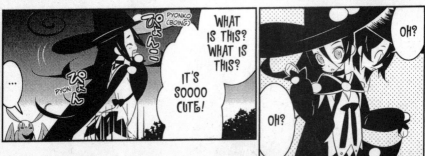

PYONKO (BOING)

WHAT IS THIS? WHAT IS THIS?

IT'S SOOOO CUTE!

...

PYON

OH?

OH?

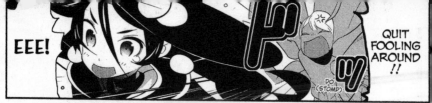

EEE!

QUIT FOOLING AROUND!!

DO (STOMP)

...

SHIIN (SILENCE)

U-UM...

CHI-CHIN PUD-DING!

ZA (SHHK)

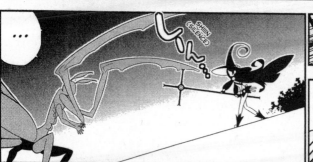

!

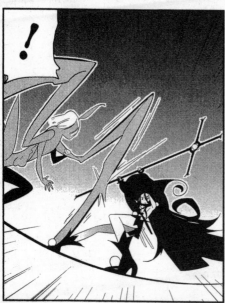

MY BODY...

KURU (SWIRL)

GAKIN (KLANG)

GO (CLOON)

DIE!!

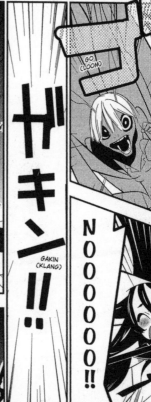

NOOOOOOO!!

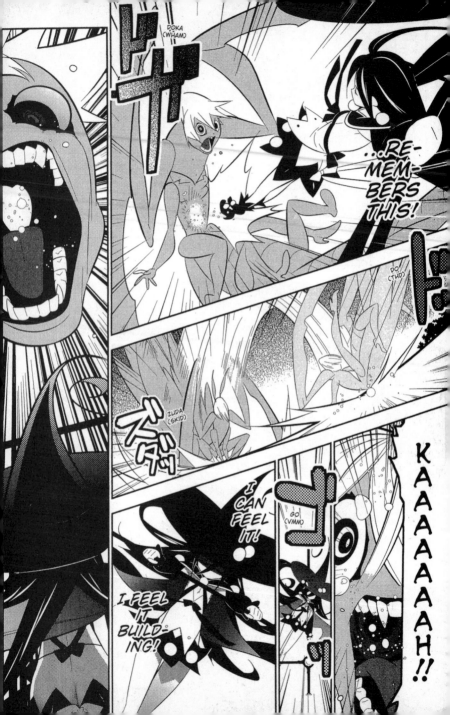

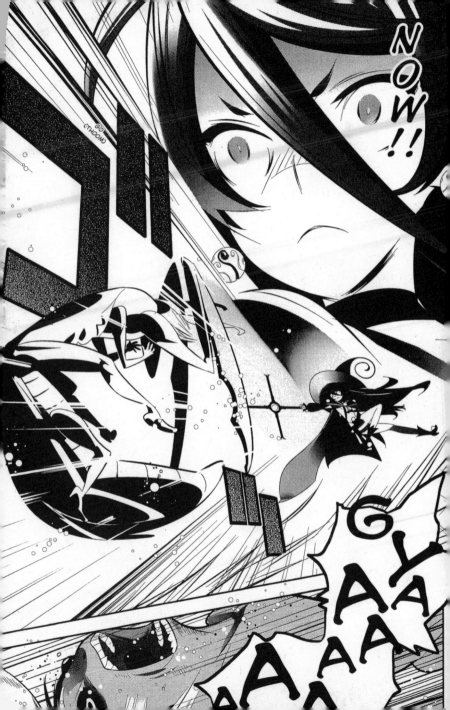

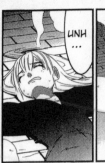

UNH ...

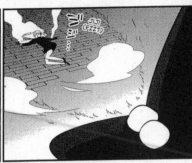

ジジ (FZZT)

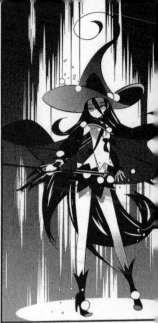

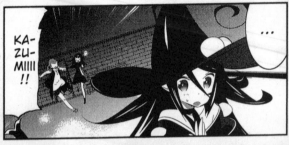

KA-ZU-MIIII!!

...

IT LOOKS LIKE ...

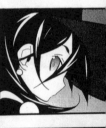

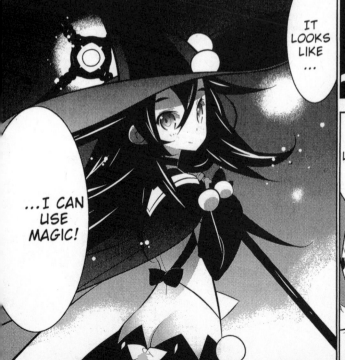

...I CAN USE MAGIC!

LISTEN!

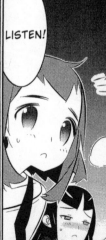

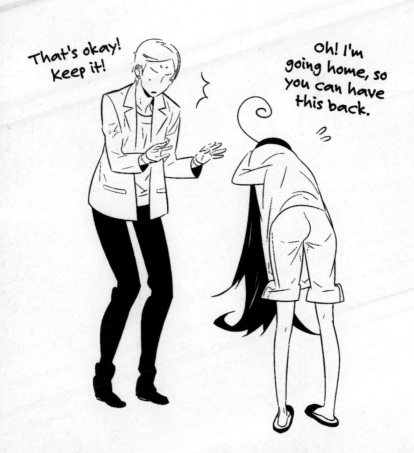

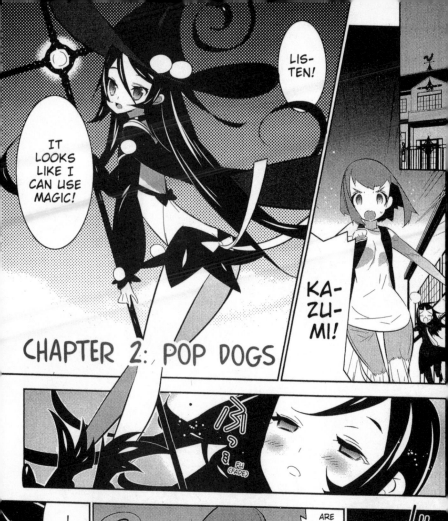

LIS-
TEN!

IT
LOOKS
LIKE I
CAN USE
MAGIC!

KA-
ZU-
MI!

CHAPTER 2: POP DOGS

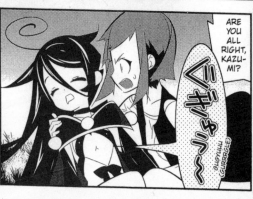

I
NEVER
HAD
DINNER
...

ARE
YOU
ALL
RIGHT,
KAZU-
MI?

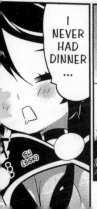

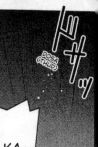

KA-
ZU-
MI!

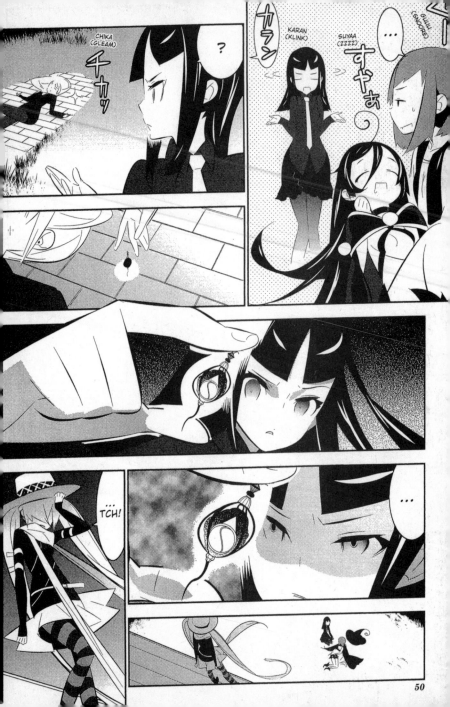

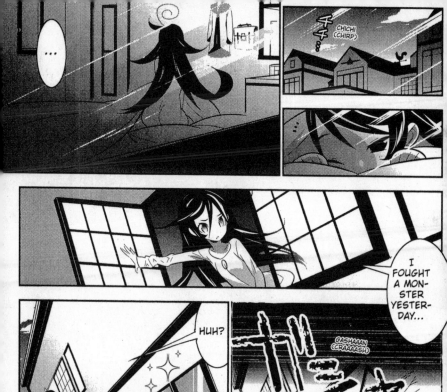

CHICHI
(CHIRP)

...

I FOUGHT A MON-STER YESTER-DAY...

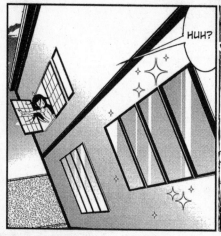

HUH?

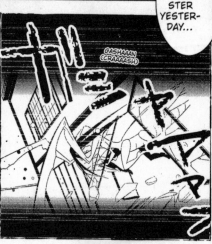

GASHAAAN
(CRAAAASH)

BUT THIS...

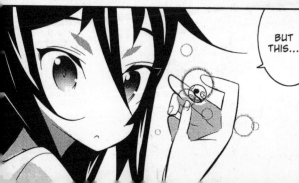

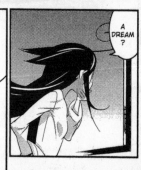

A DREAM?

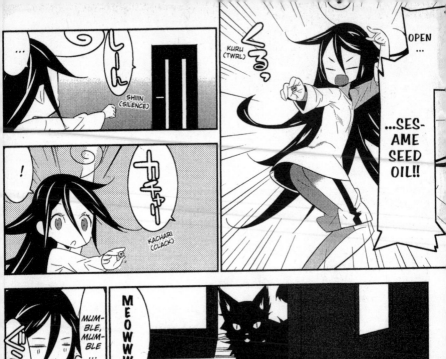

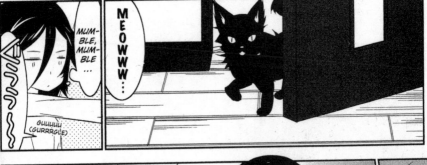

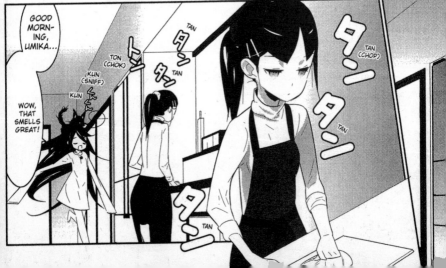

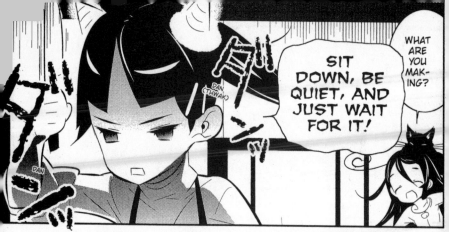

WHAT ARE YOU MAKING?

SIT DOWN, BE QUIET, AND JUST WAIT FOR IT!

DAN (THWAK)

DAN

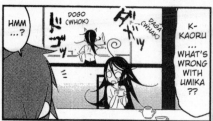

HMM...?

DOGO (WHOK)

DAGA (WHAK)

K-KAORU... WHAT'S WRONG WITH UMIKA??

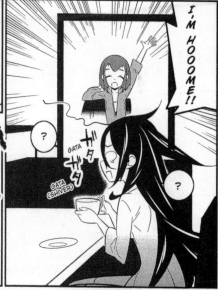

I'M HOOOME!!

?

GATA (SHIVER)

?

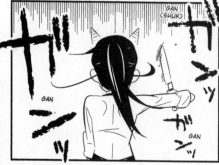

GAN (SHUK)

GAN

GAN

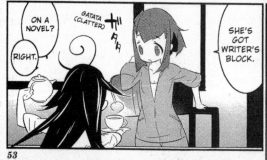

ON A NOVEL?

GATATA (CLATTER)

RIGHT.

SHE'S GOT WRITER'S BLOCK.

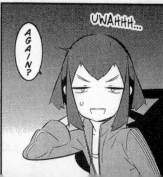

UWAHHH...

AGAIN?

53

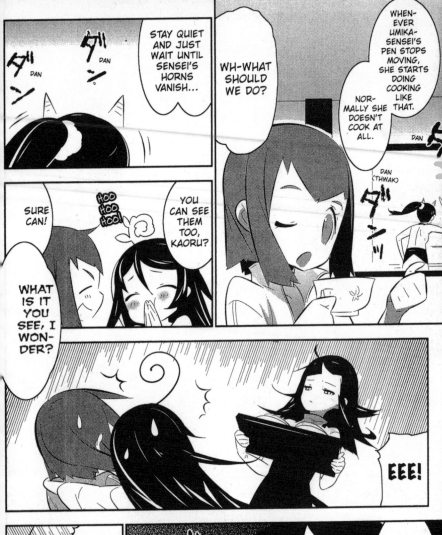
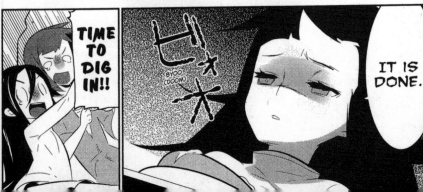

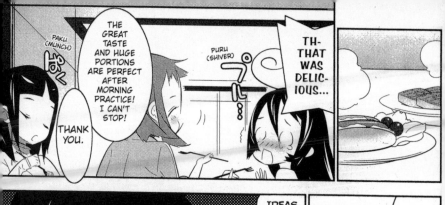

PAKU (MUNCH)

THE GREAT TASTE AND HUGE PORTIONS ARE PERFECT AFTER MORNING PRACTICE! I CAN'T STOP!

THANK YOU.

PURU (SHIVER)

TH-THAT WAS DELICIOUS...

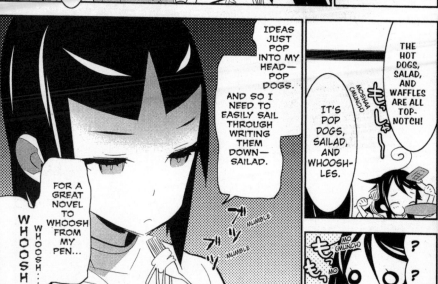

IDEAS JUST POP INTO MY HEAD— POP DOGS. AND SO I NEED TO EASILY SAIL THROUGH WRITING THEM DOWN— SAILAD.

THE HOT DOGS, SALAD, AND WAFFLES ARE ALL TOP-NOTCH!

MOSHAA (MUNCH)

IT'S POP DOGS, SAILAD, AND WHOOSH-LES.

FOR A GREAT NOVEL TO WHOOSH FROM MY PEN...

WHOOSH...
WHOOSH...
WHOOSH...

MUMBLE

MUMBLE

MO (MUNCH)

MO

?
?

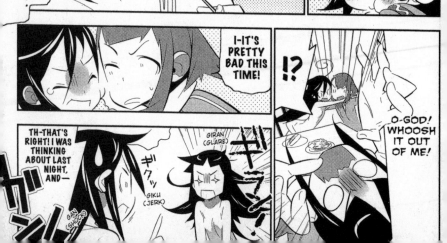

I-IT'S PRETTY BAD THIS TIME!

!?

O-GOD! WHOOSH IT OUT OF ME!

TH-THAT'S RIGHT! I WAS THINKING ABOUT LAST NIGHT, AND—

GIRAN (GLARE)

GIKU (JERK)

GAN (SHOCK)

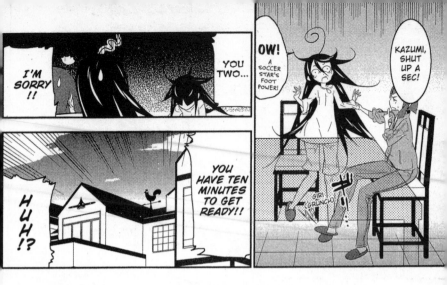

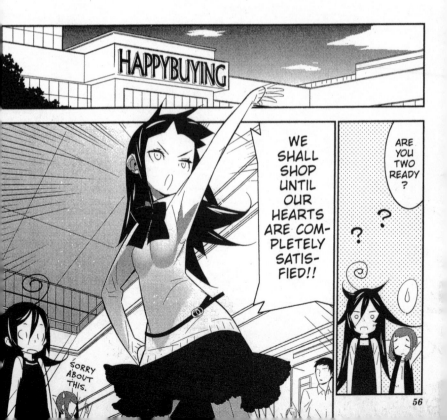

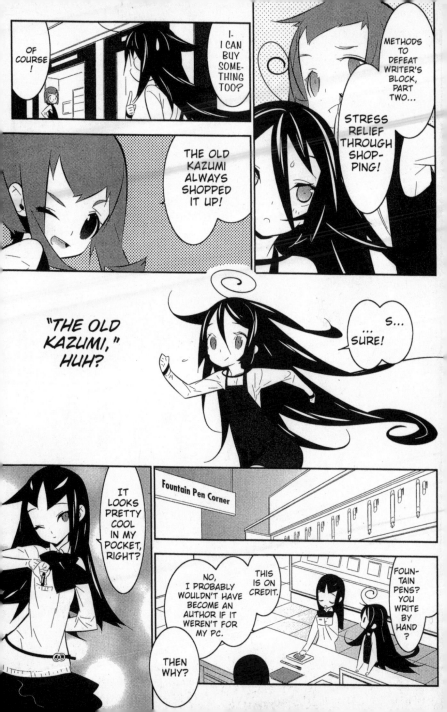

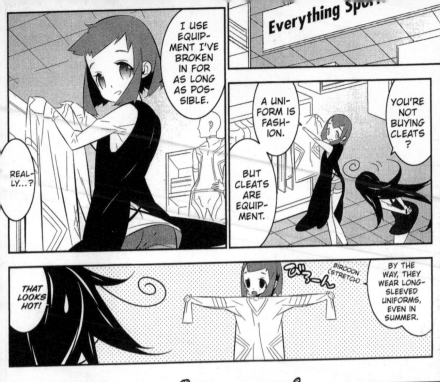

I USE EQUIPMENT I'VE BROKEN IN FOR AS LONG AS POSSIBLE.

REALLY...?

A UNIFORM IS FASHION.

BUT CLEATS ARE EQUIPMENT.

YOU'RE NOT BUYING CLEATS?

THAT LOOKS HOT!

BIROOON (STRETCH)

BY THE WAY, THEY WEAR LONG-SLEEVED UNIFORMS, EVEN IN SUMMER.

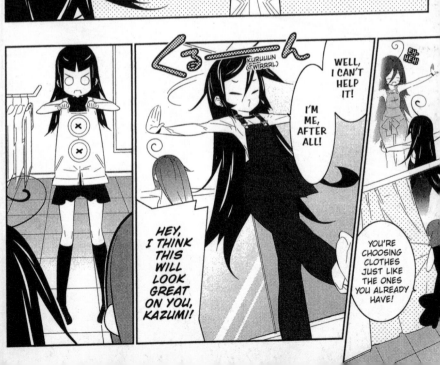

KURULULUN (TWIRRRL)

WELL, I CAN'T HELP IT!

I'M ME, AFTER ALL!

EH-HEH!

HEY, I THINK THIS WILL LOOK GREAT ON YOU, KAZUMI!

YOU'RE CHOOSING CLOTHES JUST LIKE THE ONES YOU ALREADY HAVE!

BUT TODAY'S "KAZUMI"...

...IS "THE OLD KAZUMI."

"KAZUMI," IN THE MINDS OF UMIKA AND KAORU...

WHAT'S THAT SUPPOSED TO MEAN!?

THAT'S WHY IT'D LOOK GREAT ON YOU!

...IT... LOOKS LIKE IT'S FOR KINDERGARTEN KIDS...

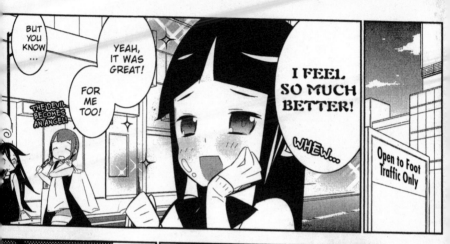

BUT YOU KNOW...

YEAH, IT WAS GREAT!

FOR ME TOO!

I FEEL SO MUCH BETTER!

WHEW...

THE DEVIL BECOMES AN ANGEL.

Open to Foot Traffic Only

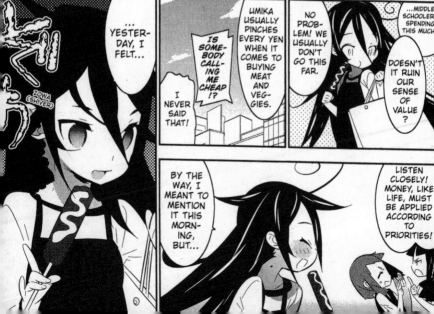

...YESTERDAY, I FELT...

ZOWA (SHIVER)

IS SOMEBODY CALLING ME CHEAP!?

I NEVER SAID THAT!

UMIKA USUALLY PINCHES EVERY YEN WHEN IT COMES TO BUYING MEAT AND VEGGIES.

NO PROBLEM! WE USUALLY DON'T GO THIS FAR.

...MIDDLE SCHOOLERS SPENDING THIS MUCH?

DOESN'T IT RUIN OUR SENSE OF VALUE?

BY THE WAY, I MEANT TO MENTION IT THIS MORNING, BUT...

LISTEN CLOSELY! MONEY, LIKE LIFE, MUST BE APPLIED ACCORDING TO PRIORITIES!

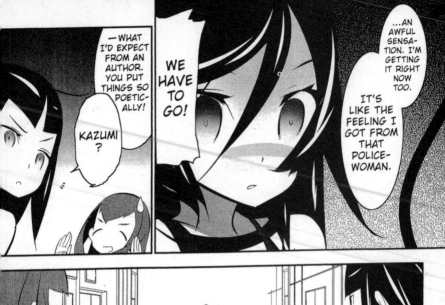

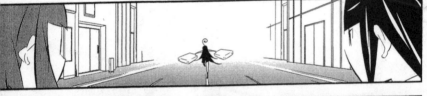

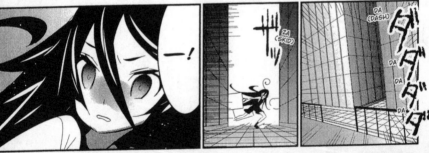

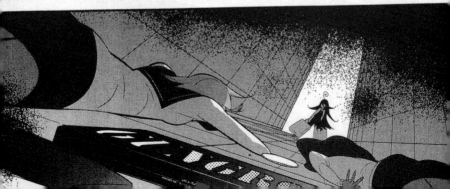

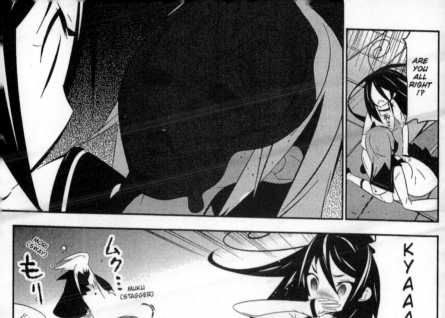

ARE YOU ALL RIGHT!?

MORI
(SWAY)

ムク...
MUKU
(STAGGER)

KYAAA!?

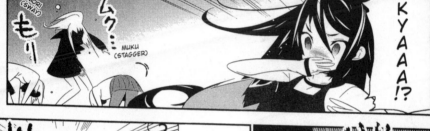

BA
(FWIP)

NOOO-OOO!!

BAA
(WHOOSH)

!

KA
(FLASH)

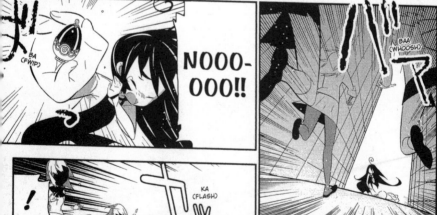

BOTA

PERI
(PEEL)

BOTA
(SPLAT)

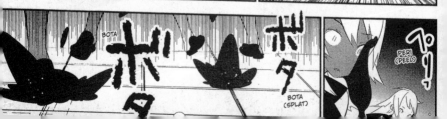

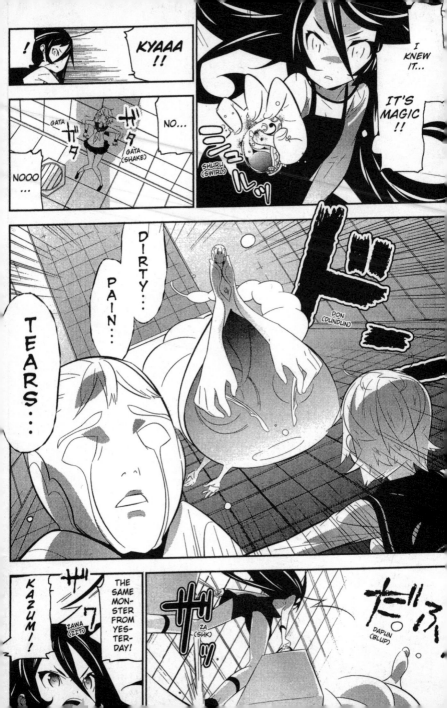

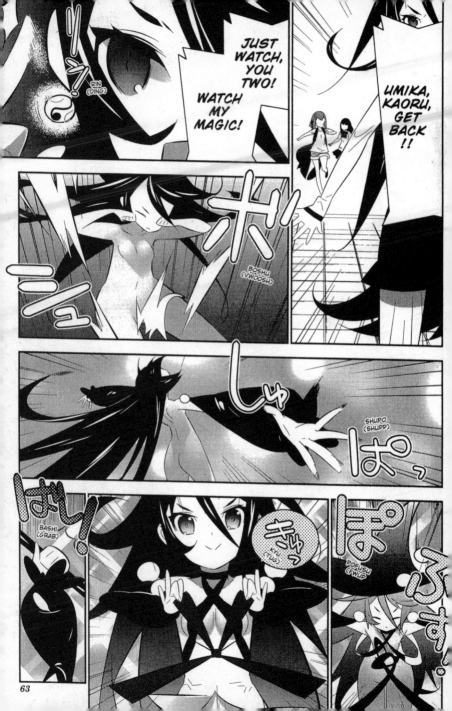

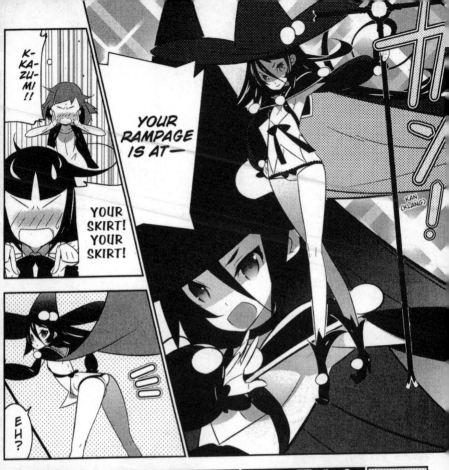

K-KA-ZU-MI!!

YOUR RAMPAGE IS AT—

YOUR SKIRT! YOUR SKIRT!

KAN (KLANG)

EH?

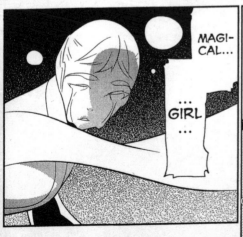

MAGI-CAL...

...GIRL...

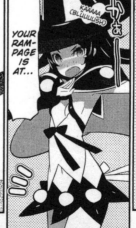

YOUR RAM-PAGE IS AT...

KAAAAA (BLUUUUSH)

TAKE TWO!

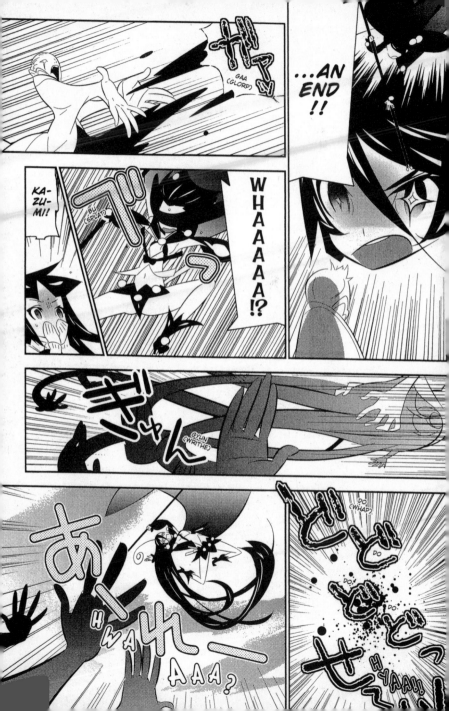

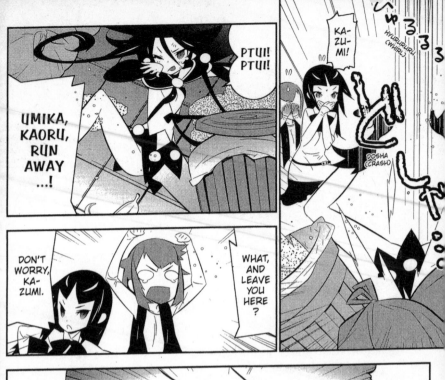

PTUI! PTUI!

UMIKA, KAORU, RUN AWAY...!

KA-ZU-MI!

HYURURURU (WHIRL)

DOSHA (CRASH)

DON'T WORRY, KA-ZUMI.

WHAT, AND LEAVE YOU HERE?

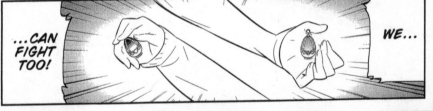

...CAN FIGHT TOO!

WE...

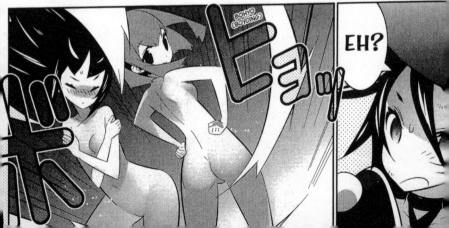

BOHYO (BOYOING?)

EH?

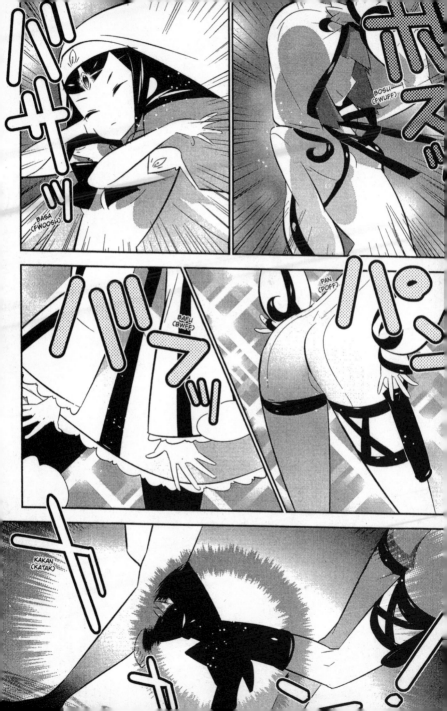

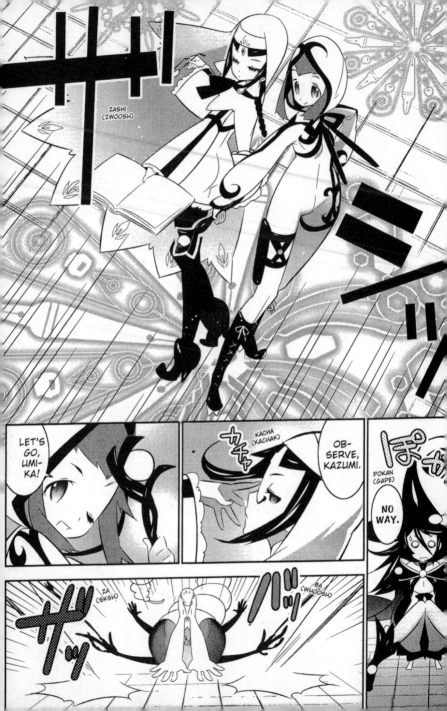

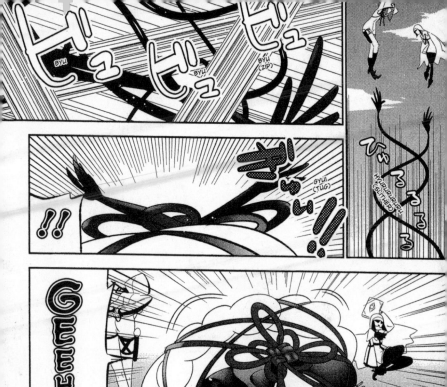

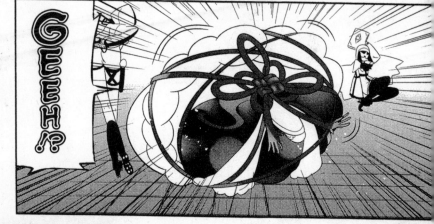

NICE
PASS
!!

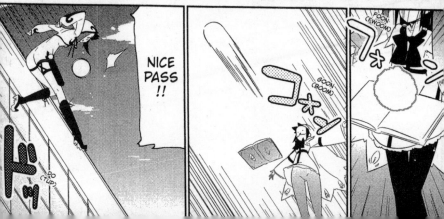

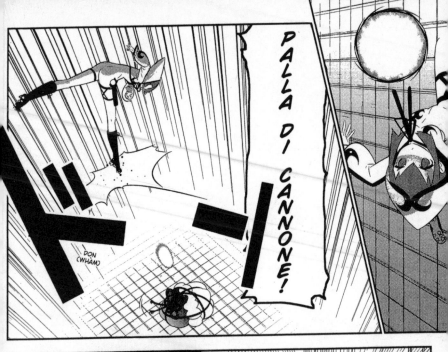

PALLA DI CANNONE!

DON
(WHAM)

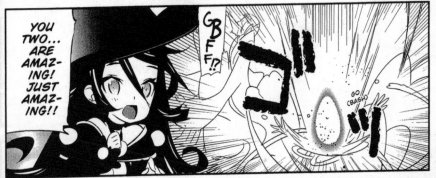

YOU TWO... ARE AMAZING! JUST AMAZING!!

GB FF!?

GO
(BASH)

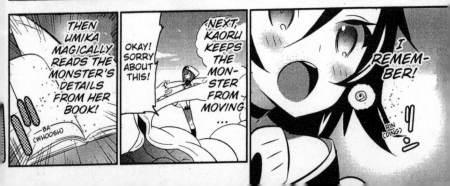

THEN UMIKA MAGICALLY READS THE MONSTER'S DETAILS FROM HER BOOK!

BA
(WHOOSH)

OKAY! SORRY ABOUT THIS!

NEXT, KAORU KEEPS THE MONSTER FROM MOVING...

I REMEMBER!

RIN
(DING)

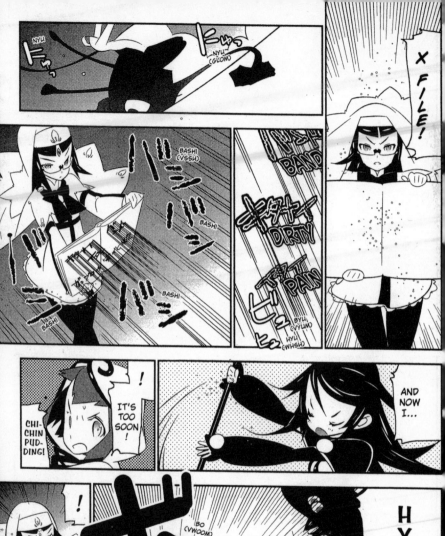

NYU (GLOM)

NYU (GLOM)

X FILE!

BASHI (VSSH)

BASHI

BASHI

BASHI

BASHI

BASH! BAND

DIRTY

PAIN

BYU (VYUM)

HYU (WHSH)

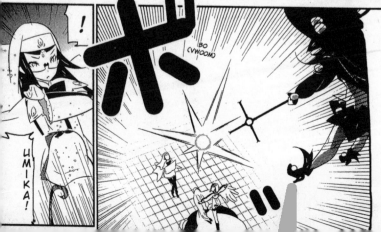

CHI-CHIN PUD-DING!

IT'S TOO SOON!

AND NOW I...

!

UMIKA!

BO (VWOOM)

HYAAAAH!!

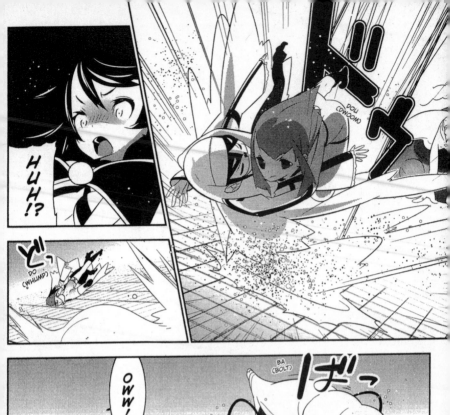

HUH!?

DOU
(DWOOM)

DO
(WHUMP)

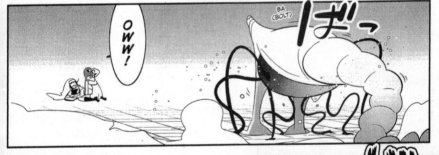

OWW!

BA
(BOLT)

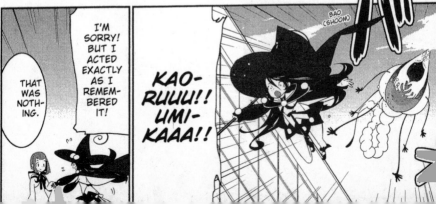

THAT WAS NOTHING.

I'M SORRY! BUT I ACTED EXACTLY AS I REMEMBERED IT!

KAO-RUUU!! UMI-KAAA!!

BAO
(SHOOM)

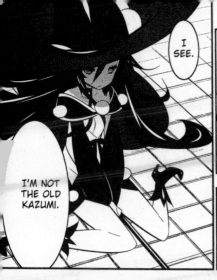

I SEE.

WE DON'T EXPECT YOU TO SUDDENLY ACT EXACLY LIKE THE OLD KAZUMI.

DON'T SWEAT IT.

I'M NOT THE OLD KAZUMI.

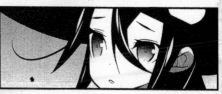

KAZUMI...

WELL, I ATTACK-ED MY FRIENDS!

WHAT I DID WAS UNFOR-GIV-ABLE!

I BEAR SOME RES-PONSIBILITY FOR ACTING WITHOUT CONSIDERING YOUR PRESENT STATE.

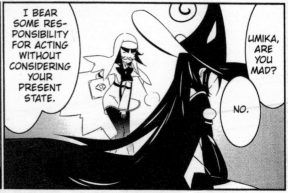

UMIKA, ARE YOU MAD?

NO.

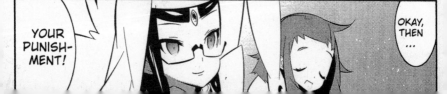

YOUR PUNISH-MENT!

OKAY, THEN ...

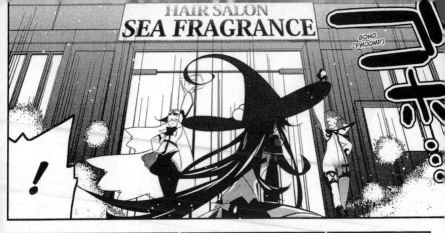

HAIR SALON
SEA FRAGRANCE

GOHO
(FWOOMP)

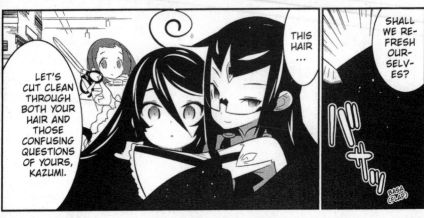

SHALL WE RE-FRESH OUR-SELV-ES?

THIS HAIR...

LET'S CUT CLEAN THROUGH BOTH YOUR HAIR AND THOSE CONFUSING QUESTIONS OF YOURS, KAZUMI.

BASA
(FLAP)

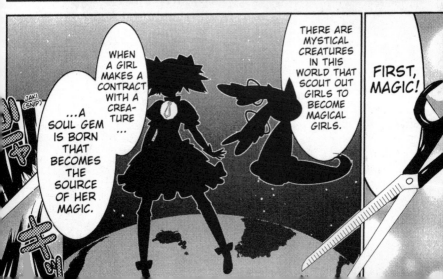

FIRST, MAGIC!

THERE ARE MYSTICAL CREATURES IN THIS WORLD THAT SCOUT OUT GIRLS TO BECOME MAGICAL GIRLS.

WHEN A GIRL MAKES A CONTRACT WITH A CREA-TURE...

...A SOUL GEM IS BORN THAT BECOMES THE SOURCE OF HER MAGIC.

JAKI
(SNIP)

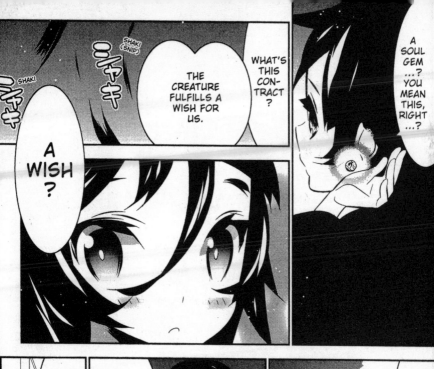

A SOUL GEM...? YOU MEAN THIS, RIGHT...?

WHAT'S THIS CONTRACT?

SHAKI

SHAKI (SNIP)

SHAKI

THE CREATURE FULFILLS A WISH FOR US.

A WISH?

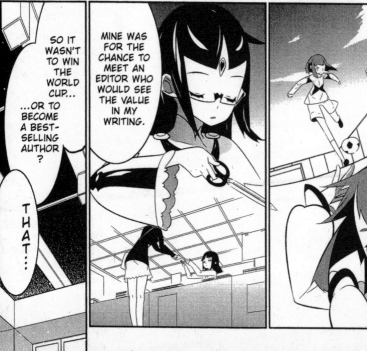

SO IT WASN'T TO WIN THE WORLD CUP... ...OR TO BECOME A BEST-SELLING AUTHOR?

THAT...

MINE WAS FOR THE CHANCE TO MEET AN EDITOR WHO WOULD SEE THE VALUE IN MY WRITING.

MINE WAS TO HAVE A BODY STRONG ENOUGH TO BE A TOP-CLASS SOCCER PLAYER.

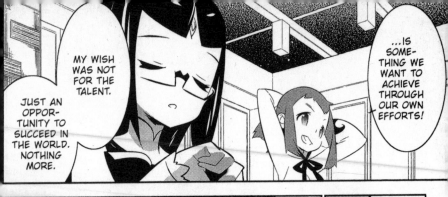

MY WISH WAS NOT FOR THE TALENT.

JUST AN OPPORTUNITY TO SUCCEED IN THE WORLD. NOTHING MORE.

...IS SOMETHING WE WANT TO ACHIEVE THROUGH OUR OWN EFFORTS!

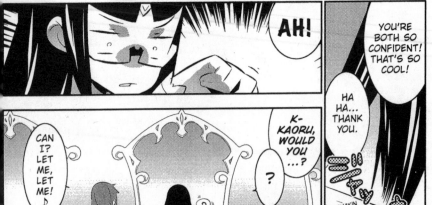

AH!

YOU'RE BOTH SO CONFIDENT! THAT'S SO COOL!

HA HA... THANK YOU.

SHAKIN (SNKK)

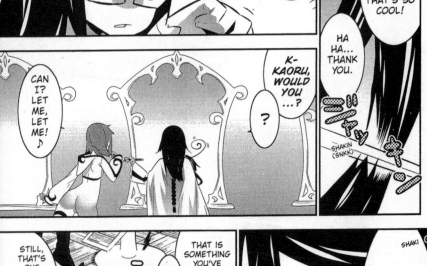

CAN I? LET ME, LET ME! ♪

K-KAORU, WOULD YOU...?

?

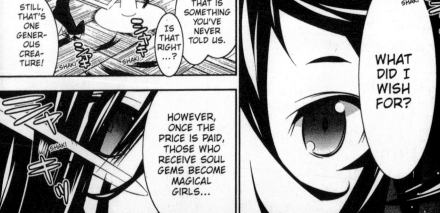

STILL, THAT'S ONE GENEROUS CREATURE!

THAT IS SOMETHING YOU'VE NEVER TOLD US.

IS THAT RIGHT...?

SHAKI!

SHAKI!

SHAKI!

HOWEVER, ONCE THE PRICE IS PAID, THOSE WHO RECEIVE SOUL GEMS BECOME MAGICAL GIRLS...

SHAKI!

SHAKI

WHAT DID I WISH FOR?

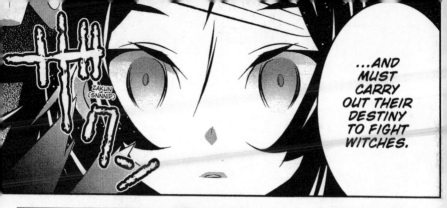

...AND MUST CARRY OUT THEIR DESTINY TO FIGHT WITCHES.

ZAKUN (SNNNIP)

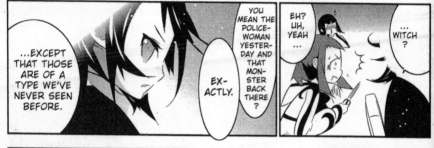

...EXCEPT THAT THOSE ARE OF A TYPE WE'VE NEVER SEEN BEFORE.

EX-ACTLY.

YOU MEAN THE POLICE-WOMAN YESTER-DAY AND THAT MON-STER BACK THERE?

EH? UH, YEAH...

...WITCH?

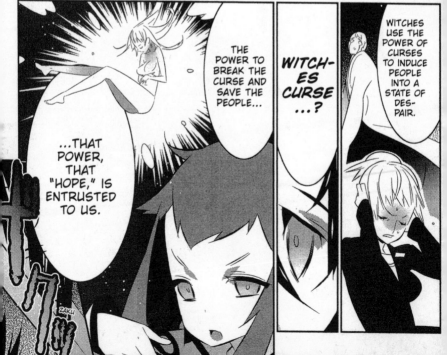

THE POWER TO BREAK THE CURSE AND SAVE THE PEOPLE...

...THAT POWER, THAT "HOPE," IS ENTRUSTED TO US.

WITCH-ES CURSE ...?

WITCHES USE THE POWER OF CURSES TO INDUCE PEOPLE INTO A STATE OF DES-PAIR.

ZAKU

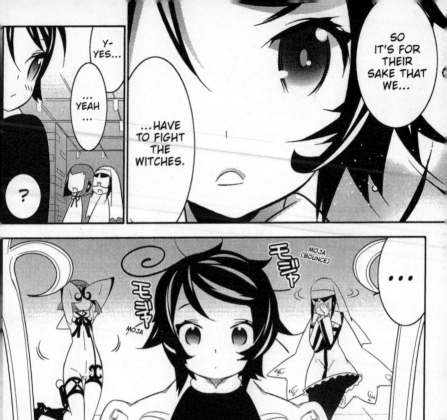
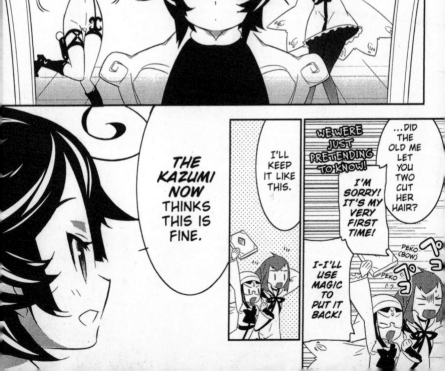

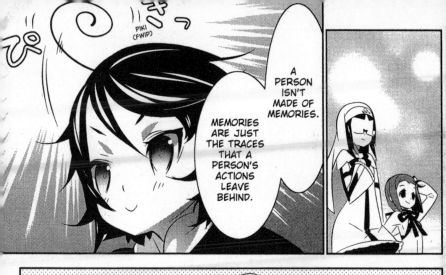

PIKI
(FWIP)

A PERSON ISN'T MADE OF MEMORIES.

MEMORIES ARE JUST THE TRACES THAT A PERSON'S ACTIONS LEAVE BEHIND.

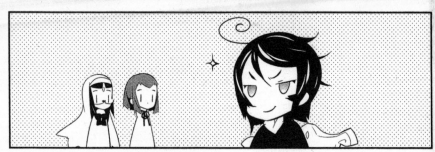

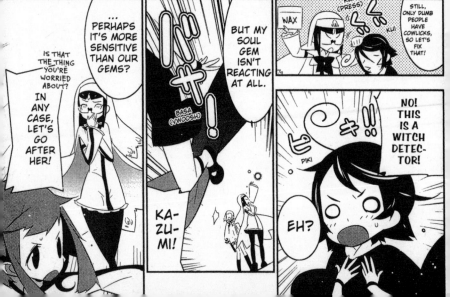

IS THAT THE THING YOU'RE WORRIED ABOUT?

IN ANY CASE, LET'S GO AFTER HER!

...PERHAPS IT'S MORE SENSITIVE THAN OUR GEMS?

BUT MY SOUL GEM ISN'T REACTING AT ALL.

BASA
(VWOOSH)

KA-ZU-MI!

WAX

KUI
(PRESS)

KUI

STILL, ONLY DUMB PEOPLE HAVE COWLICKS, SO LET'S FIX THAT!

NO! THIS IS A WITCH DETECTOR!

PIKI

EH?

IT GIVES ME THE SHIVERS, BUT I DON'T THINK SO.

KAZUMI, IS THIS THE PLACE?

IF WE WORK BACKWARD FROM HERE...

...WE MAY BE ABLE TO DETERMINE WHERE THE WITCH WILL STRIKE NEXT.

WITCHES TEND TO FOLLOW CERTAIN PATTERNS WHEN ATTACKING HUMANS.

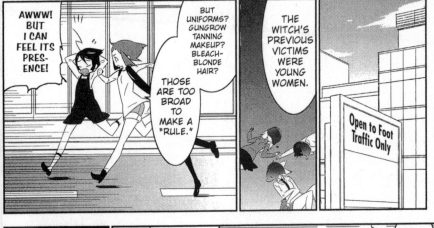

AWWW! BUT I CAN FEEL ITS PRESENCE!

BUT UNIFORMS? GUNGROW TANNING MAKEUP? BLEACH-BLONDE HAIR?

THOSE ARE TOO BROAD TO MAKE A "RULE."

THE WITCH'S PREVIOUS VICTIMS WERE YOUNG WOMEN.

Open to Foot Traffic Only

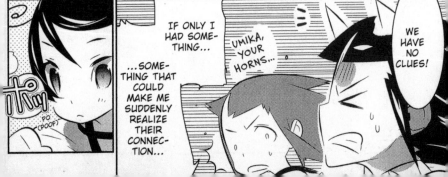

IF ONLY I HAD SOME-THING...

...SOME-THING THAT COULD MAKE ME SUDDENLY REALIZE THEIR CONNEC-TION...

UMIKA, YOUR HORNS...

WE HAVE NO CLUES!

PO (POOF)

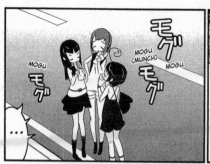 モグ MOGU

MOGU (MUNCH) モグ モグ

...

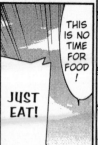 THIS IS NO TIME FOR FOOD!

JUST EAT!

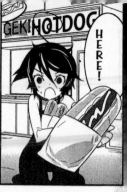 GEKI HOTDOG

HERE!

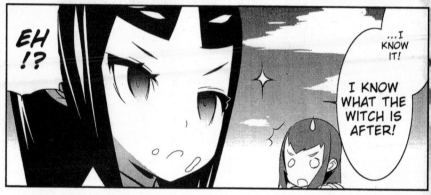 EH!?

...I KNOW IT!

I KNOW WHAT THE WITCH IS AFTER!

Live Demonstration Event

GUNGROW

Gun Gro

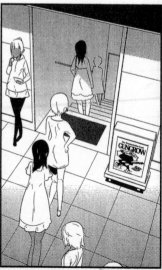 GUNGROW

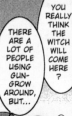 THERE ARE A LOT OF PEOPLE USING GUN-GROW AROUND, BUT...

YOU REALLY THINK THE WITCH WILL COME HERE?

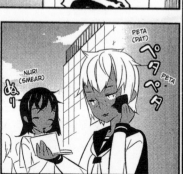 PETA (PAT) ペタ

ペタ PETA

NURI (SMEAR) ぬり

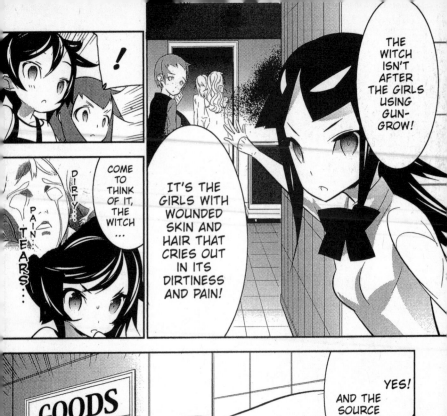

THE WITCH ISN'T AFTER THE GIRLS USING GUN-GROW!

IT'S THE GIRLS WITH WOUNDED SKIN AND HAIR THAT CRIES OUT IN ITS DIRTINESS AND PAIN!

COME TO THINK OF IT, THE WITCH...

DIRTY...

PAIN...

TEARS...

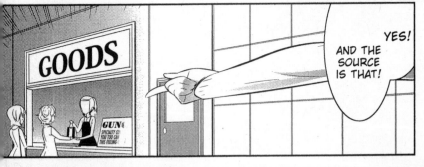

GOODS

GUN
SPECIALTY CO
THIS FEELING

YES! AND THE SOURCE IS THAT!

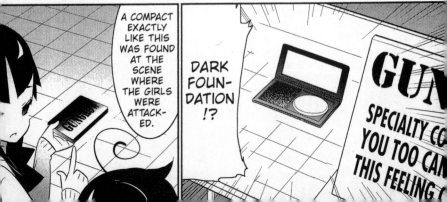

A COMPACT EXACTLY LIKE THIS WAS FOUND AT THE SCENE WHERE THE GIRLS WERE ATTACK-ED.

DARK FOUN-DATION!?

GUN
SPECIALTY CO
YOU TOO CA
THIS FEELING

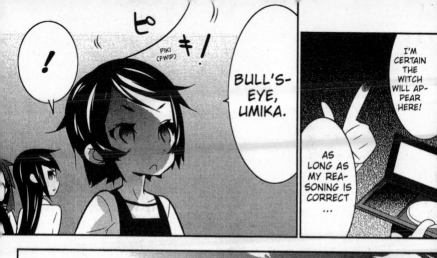

！

ピ
キ！

PIKI
(FWIP)

BULL'S-EYE, UMIKA.

I'M CERTAIN THE WITCH WILL APPEAR HERE!

AS LONG AS MY REASONING IS CORRECT...

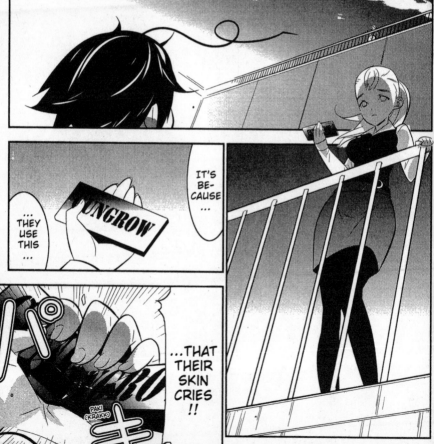

IT'S BECAUSE...

...THEY USE THIS...

UNGROW

...THAT THEIR SKIN CRIES!!

パ
キ

PAKI
(KRAK)

I'LL TEACH THEM...

...THE PROPER APPLICATION OF COSMETICS!

グニュ
GUNYU (OOZE)

I'LL TEACH THEM THAT!

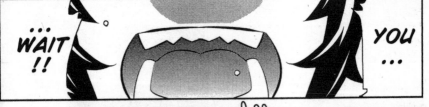

WAIT!!

YOU...

...YOU CAN'T GO AROUND ATTACKING PEOPLE!!

ZA (ZSH)

JUST BECAUSE THEY USE GUNGROW AND RUIN THEIR SKIN...

AND LOOK LIKE SLOBS WHEN THEY CRUSH THE BACKS OF THEIR SHOES SLIPPING THEM ON...

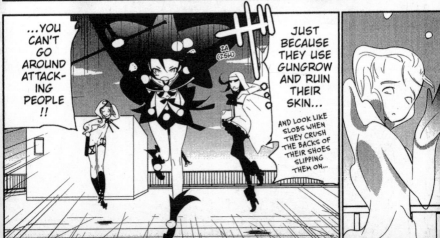

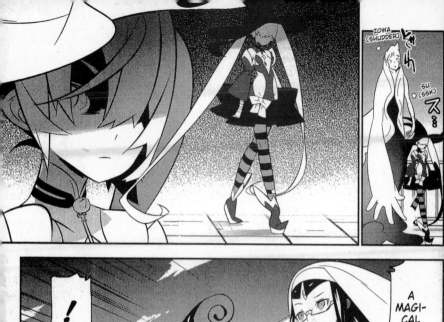

ZOWA
(SHUDDER)

SU
(SSK)

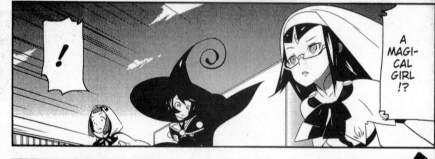

A
MAGI-
CAL
GIRL
!?

!

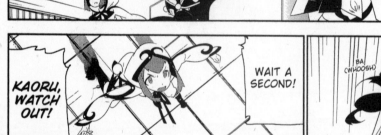

KAORU,
WATCH
OUT!

WAIT A
SECOND!

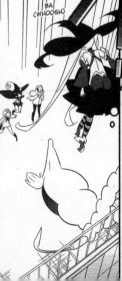

BA
(WHOOSH)

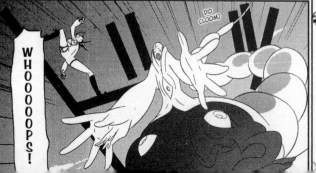

WHOOOOOPS!

DO
(LOOM)

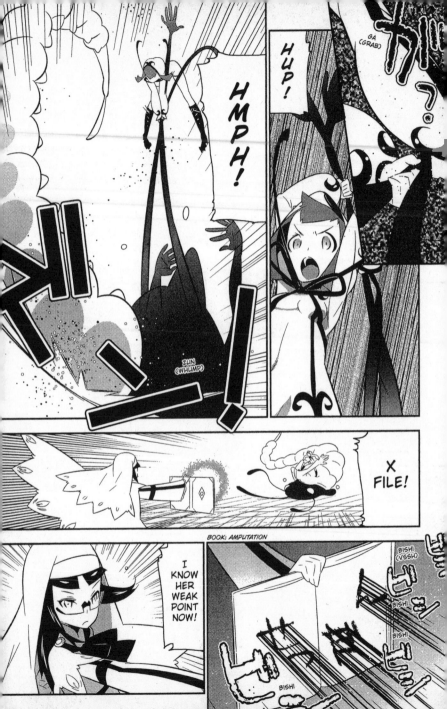

BOOK: AMPUTATION

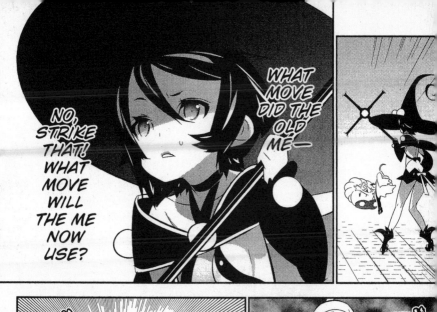

NO, STRIKE THAT! WHAT MOVE WILL THE ME NOW USE?

WHAT MOVE DID THE OLD ME—

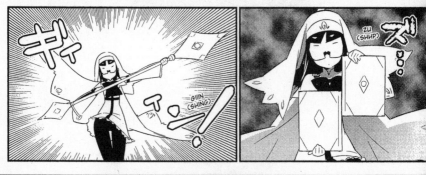

ギィ

イ

GIIN (SHING)

ズ

ズ

ZU (SHHP)

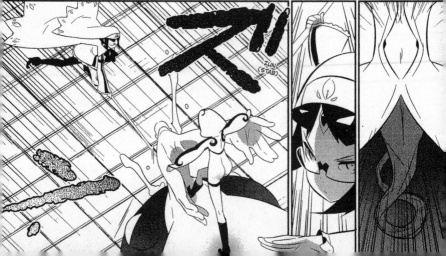

ズ

ズン (STAB)

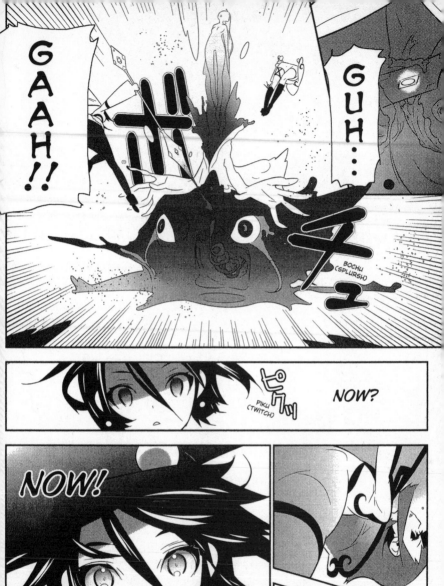

GAAH!!

GUH...

BOCHU
(SPLURSH)

PIKU
(TWITCH)

NOW?

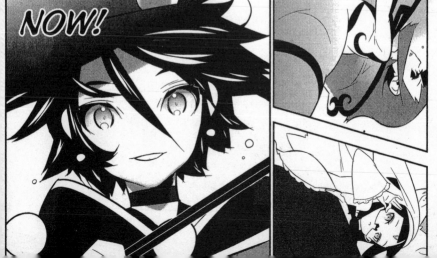

NOW!

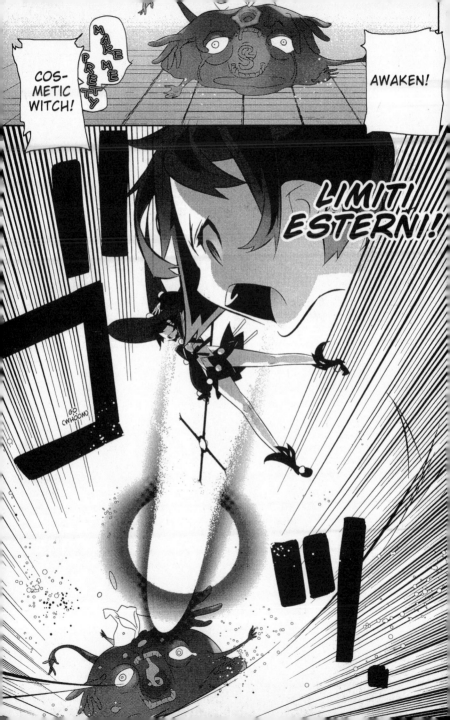

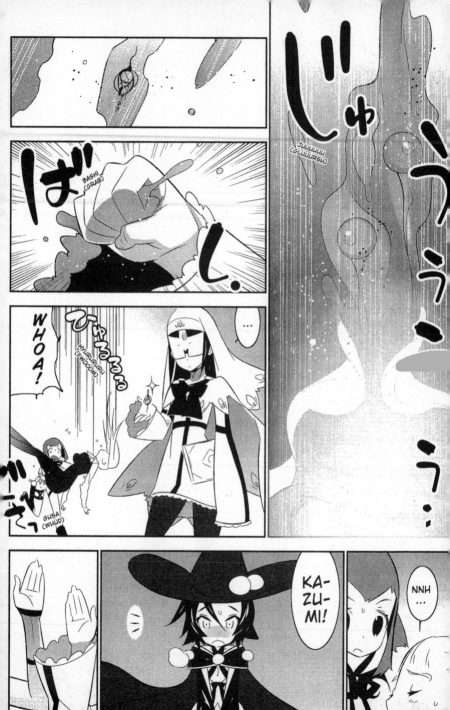

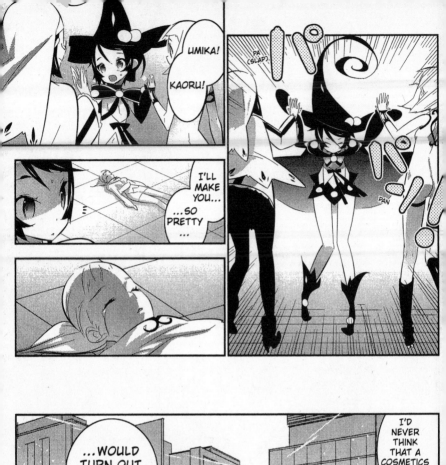
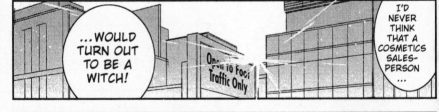
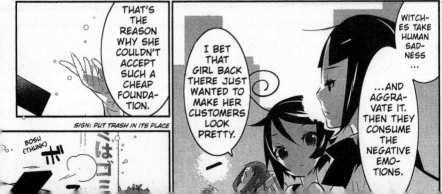

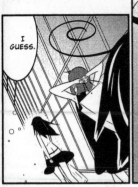

I GUESS.

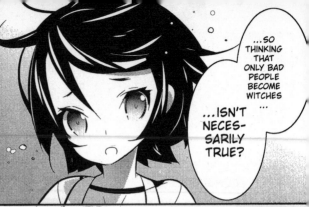

...SO THINKING THAT ONLY BAD PEOPLE BECOME WITCHES...

...ISN'T NECESSARILY TRUE?

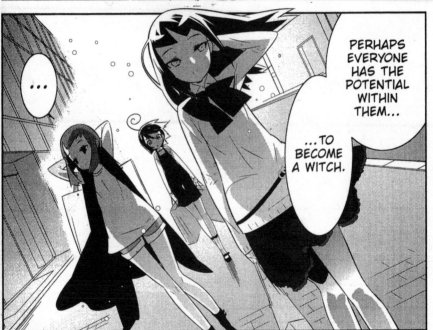

· · ·

PERHAPS EVERYONE HAS THE POTENTIAL WITHIN THEM...

...TO BECOME A WITCH.

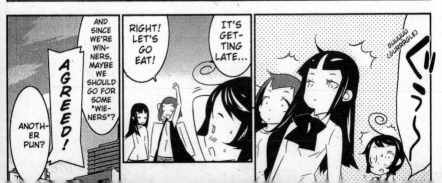

ANOTHER PUN?

AGREED!

AND SINCE WE'RE WINNERS, MAYBE WE SHOULD GO FOR SOME "WIENERS"?

RIGHT! LET'S GO EAT!

IT'S GETTING LATE...

GUUUUU (GURRRGLE)

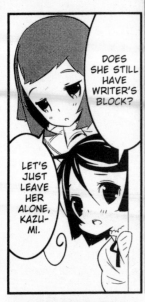

DOES SHE STILL HAVE WRITER'S BLOCK?

LET'S JUST LEAVE HER ALONE, KAZUMI.

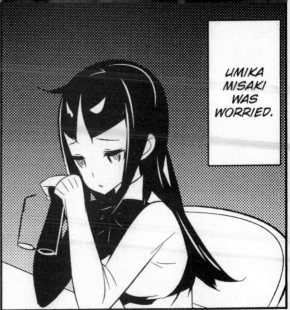

UMIKA MISAKI WAS WORRIED.

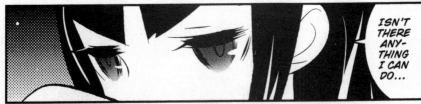

ISN'T THERE ANYTHING I CAN DO...

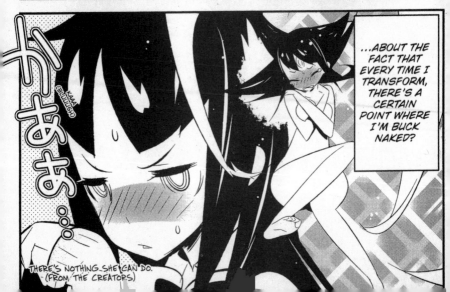

...ABOUT THE FACT THAT EVERY TIME I TRANSFORM, THERE'S A CERTAIN POINT WHERE I'M BUCK NAKED?

KAA (GUUUUSH)

THERE'S NOTHING SHE CAN DO. (FROM THE CREATORS)

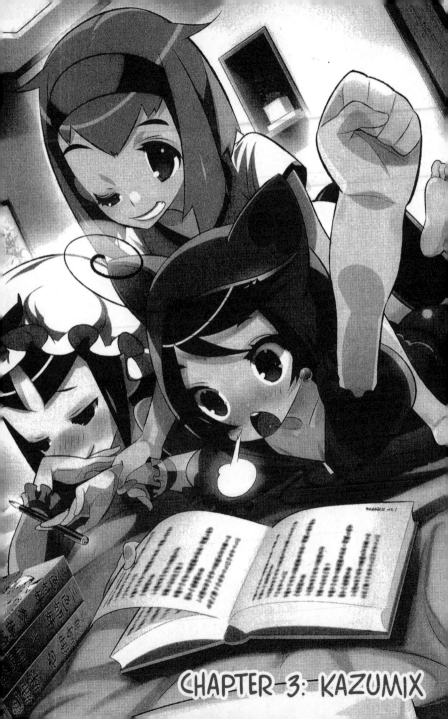

CHAPTER 3: KAZUMIX

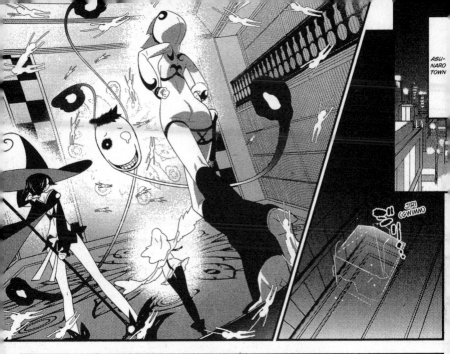

ASU-
NARO
TOWN

JIRI
(GWIMM)

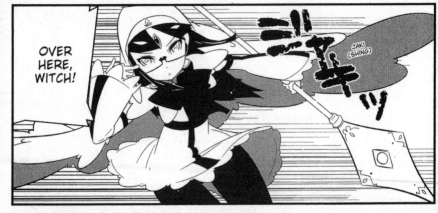

OVER
HERE,
WITCH!

JAKI
(SHING)

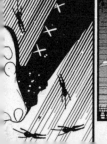

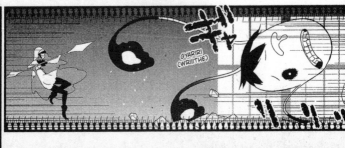

GYARIRI
(WRIIITHE)

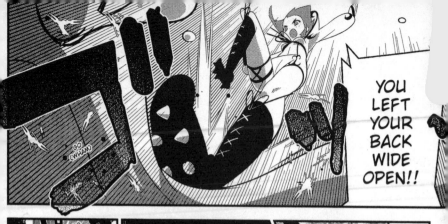

YOU LEFT YOUR BACK WIDE OPEN!!

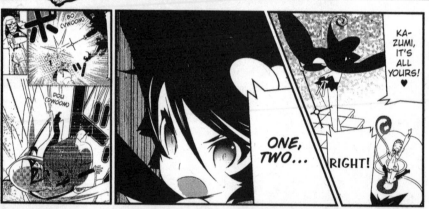

KAZUMI, IT'S ALL YOURS! ♥

ONE, TWO...

RIGHT!

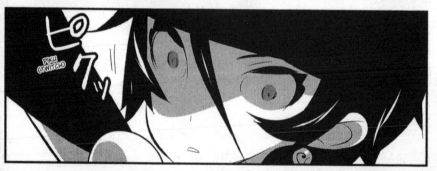

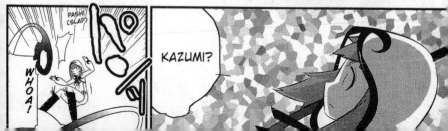

KAZUMI?

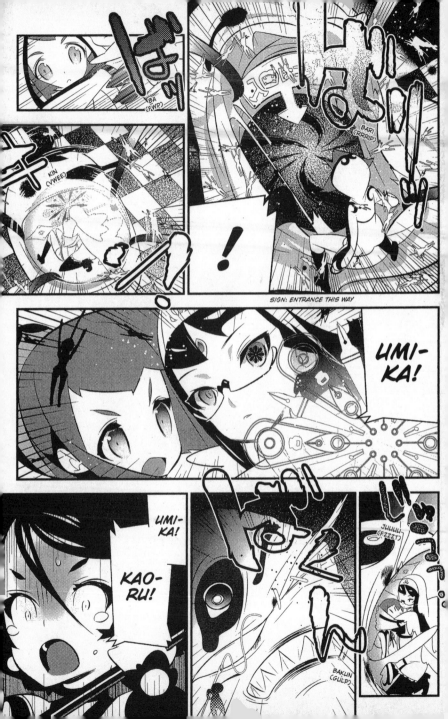

SIGN: ENTRANCE THIS WAY

UMI-KA!

UMI-KA!

KAO-RU!

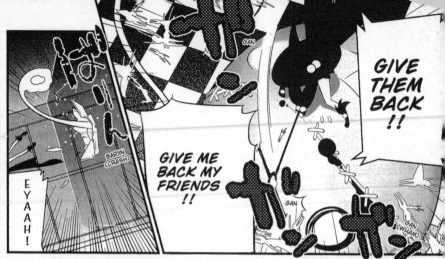

GIVE THEM BACK!!

GIVE ME BACK MY FRIENDS!!

BARIIN (CRASH)

EYAAH!

GAN

GAN

GAN (GWHAM)

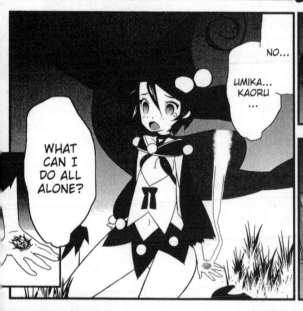

NO...

UMIKA... KAORU...

WHAT CAN I DO ALL ALONE?

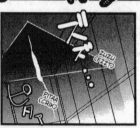

ZUZU (FZZZ)

PITAN (CRIK)

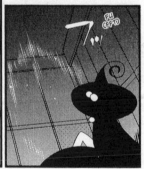

PLI (FFFP)

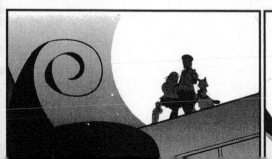

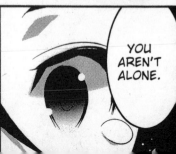

YOU AREN'T ALONE.

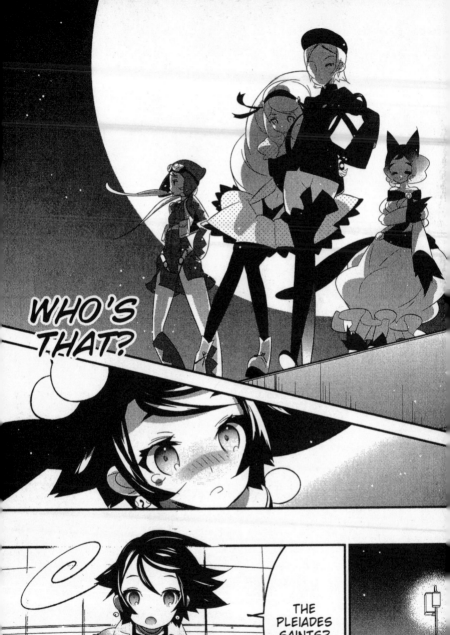

WHO'S THAT?

THE PLEIADES SAINTS?

THE SEVEN OF US FORMED A TEAM TO TAKE ON WITCHES.

YES.

THE FOUR OF US ALONG WITH YOU THREE, KAZUMI-CHAN.

THOSE SEVEN STARS UP THERE!

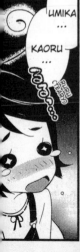

UMIKA...

KAORU...

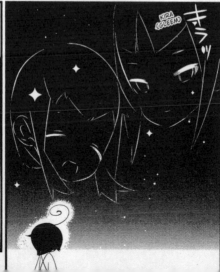

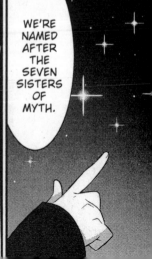

WE'RE NAMED AFTER THE SEVEN SISTERS OF MYTH.

KIRA (GLEEM)

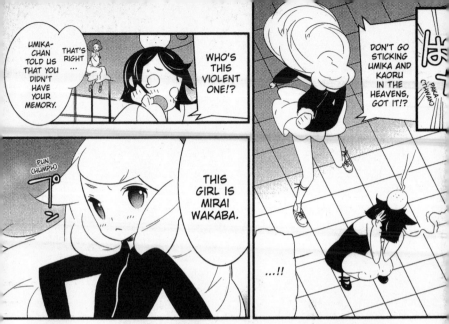

UMIKA-CHAN TOLD US THAT YOU DIDN'T HAVE YOUR MEMORY.

THAT'S RIGHT...

WHO'S THIS VIOLENT ONE!?

DON'T GO STICKING UMIKA AND KAORU IN THE HEAVENS, GOT IT!?

PIKA (TWHACK)

PUN (CHUMP!!)

THIS GIRL IS MIRAI WAKABA.

...!!

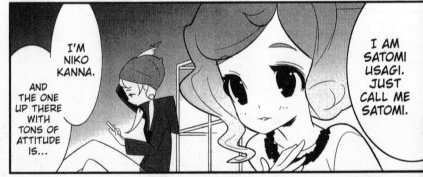

I'M NIKO KANNA.

AND THE ONE UP THERE WITH TONS OF ATTITUDE IS...

I AM SATOMI USAGI. JUST CALL ME SATOMI.

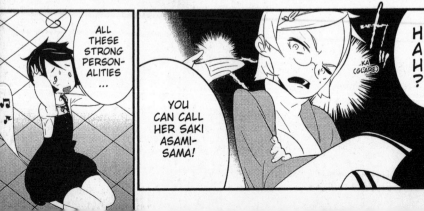

ALL THESE STRONG PERSONAL- ITIES...

YOU CAN CALL HER SAKI ASAMI- SAMA!

KA (GLARE)

H A H ?

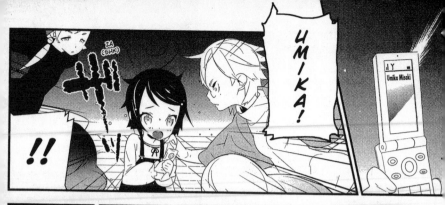
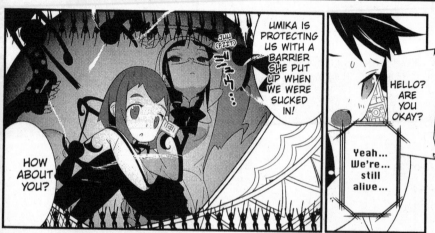
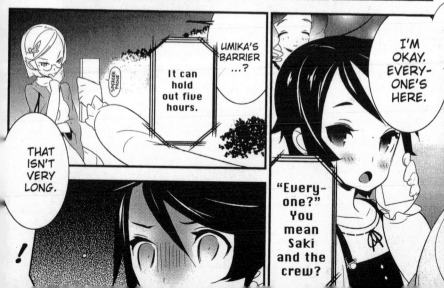

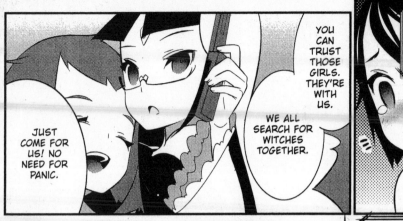

YOU CAN TRUST THOSE GIRLS. THEY'RE WITH US.

WE ALL SEARCH FOR WITCHES TOGETHER.

JUST COME FOR US! NO NEED FOR PANIC.

Ka-zumi?

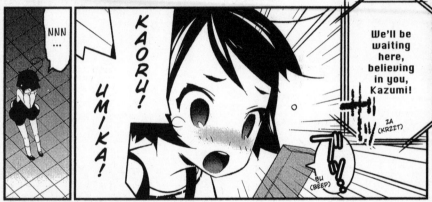

NNN...

KAORU!

UMIKA!

We'll be waiting here, believing in you, Kazumi!

ZA (KRZZT)

BU (BEEP)

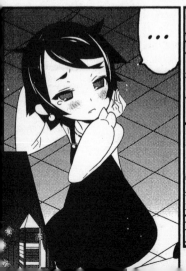

...

YOU'D BETTER, 'COS WE'RE THE ONLY PEOPLE WHO CAN SAVE THOSE TWO!!

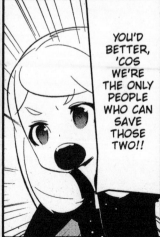

PAKO (THWAK)

PULL YOUR-SELF TO-GETHER, IDIOT!

AGAIN...?

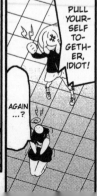

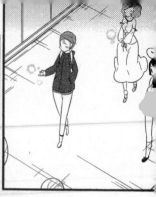

WHAT'S THIS?

WE'RE SEARCHING FOR THE WITCH.

YEAH... THE GEM ISN'T JUST AN ITEM FOR TRANSFORMING, IT'S A WITCH DETECTOR.

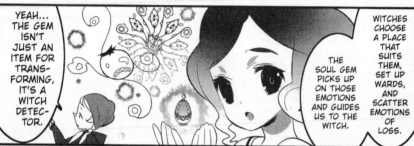

THE SOUL GEM PICKS UP ON THOSE EMOTIONS AND GUIDES US TO THE WITCH.

WITCHES CHOOSE A PLACE THAT SUITS THEM, SET UP WARDS, AND SCATTER EMOTIONS OF LOSS.

THEIR GEMS ARE WORKING, SO WHY ISN'T MY OWN SEARCH DEVICE REACTING?

TYPICAL. THIS ISN'T REGISTERING ENOUGH.

I WISH WE HAD SOME HELP HERE.

SHIIN (SILENT)

SO WE'RE SEARCHING FOR CLUES TO FIND UMIKA AND KAORU?

IF WE CAN GATHER ENOUGH DATA TO MAKE A DEDUCTION.

THIS LAST TIME, YOU FOUND THE WITCH BY ACCIDENT, RIGHT? USING THE GEM IS A MORE ASSURED METHOD.

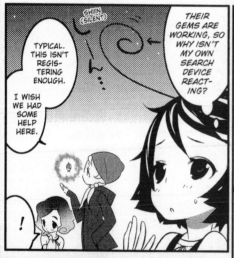

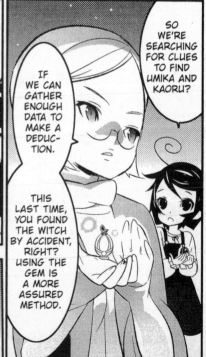

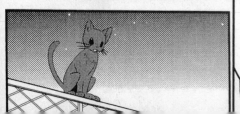

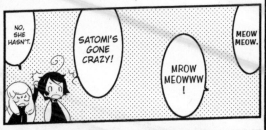

NO, SHE HASN'T.

SATOMI'S GONE CRAZY!

MROW MEOWWW!

MEOW MEOW.

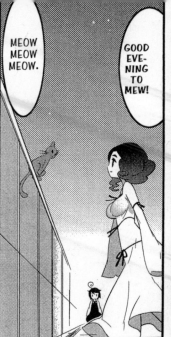

MEOW MEOW MEOW.

GOOD EVENING TO MEW!

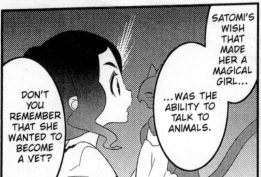

DON'T YOU REMEMBER THAT SHE WANTED TO BECOME A VET?

SATOMI'S WISH THAT MADE HER A MAGICAL GIRL...

...WAS THE ABILITY TO TALK TO ANIMALS.

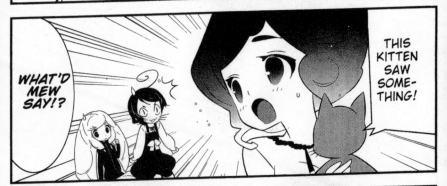

WHAT'D MEW SAY!?

THIS KITTEN SAW SOMETHING!

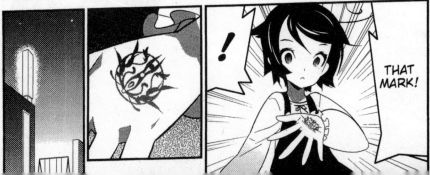

!

THAT MARK!

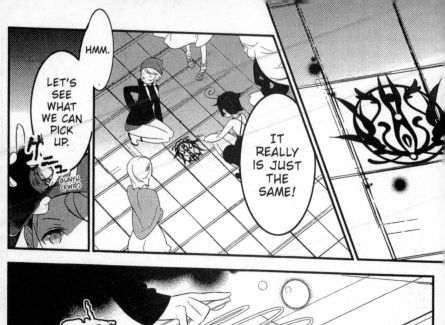

HMM.

LET'S SEE WHAT WE CAN PICK UP.

IT REALLY IS JUST THE SAME!

GUNYU (FWIP)

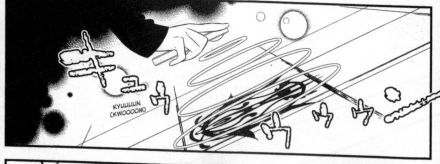

KYUUUUUN (KWOOOOM)

YOUR GEMS, EVERY- BODY.

OKAY.

SHE HAS AN APP SHE PROGRAMMED TO SUCK UP THE REMAINING TRACES OF WITCHES.

?

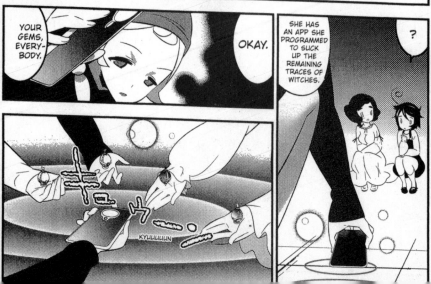

KYUUUUUN

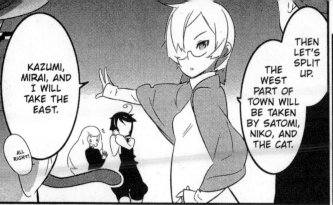

KAZUMI, MIRAI, AND I WILL TAKE THE EAST.

THE WEST PART OF TOWN WILL BE TAKEN BY SATOMI, NIKO, AND THE CAT.

THEN LET'S SPLIT UP.

ALL RIGHT!

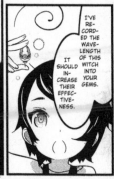

I'VE RECORDED THE WAVELENGTH OF THIS WITCH INTO YOUR GEMS.

IT SHOULD INCREASE THEIR EFFECTIVENESS.

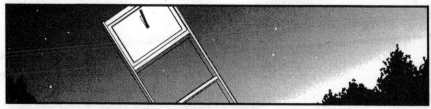

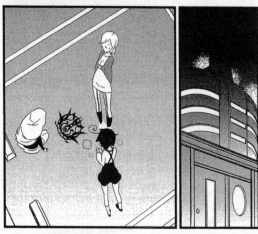

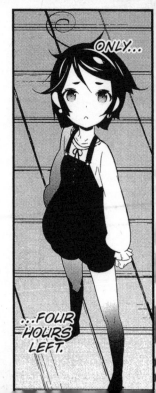

ONLY...

...FOUR HOURS LEFT.

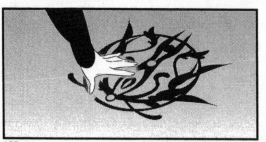

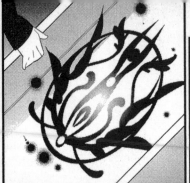
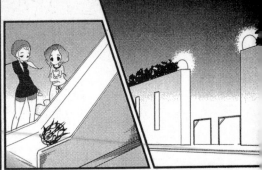
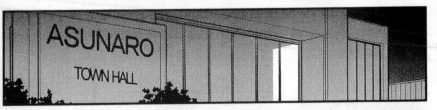
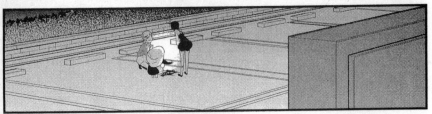
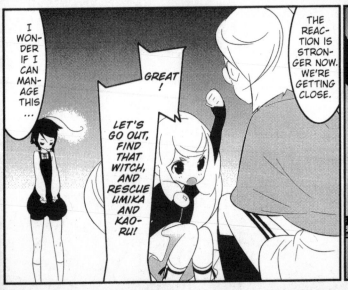
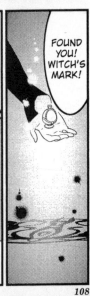

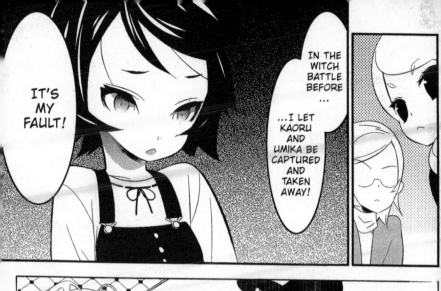

IN THE WITCH BATTLE BEFORE...

...I LET KAORU AND UMIKA BE CAPTURED AND TAKEN AWAY!

IT'S MY FAULT!

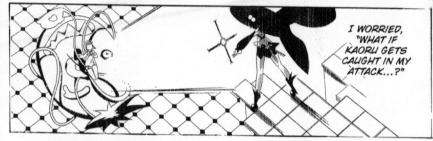

I WORRIED, "WHAT IF KAORU GETS CAUGHT IN MY ATTACK...?"

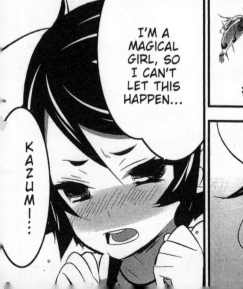

I'M A MAGICAL GIRL, SO I CAN'T LET THIS HAPPEN...

KAZUMI...!

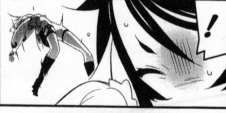

!

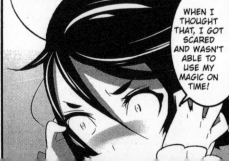

WHEN I THOUGHT THAT, I GOT SCARED AND WASN'T ABLE TO USE MY MAGIC ON TIME!

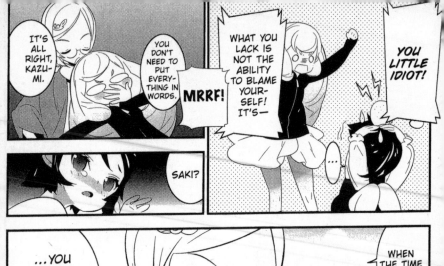

IT'S ALL RIGHT, KAZUMI.

YOU DON'T NEED TO PUT EVERYTHING IN WORDS.

MRRF!

WHAT YOU LACK IS NOT THE ABILITY TO BLAME YOURSELF! IT'S—

YOU LITTLE IDIOT!

...

SAKI?

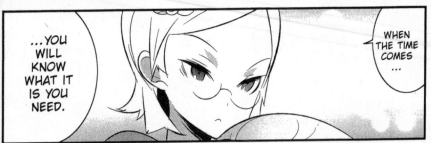

...YOU WILL KNOW WHAT IT IS YOU NEED.

WHEN THE TIME COMES...

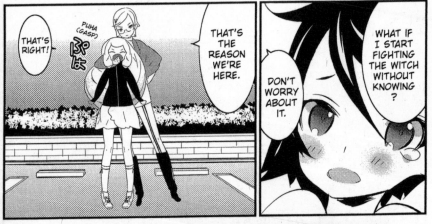

THAT'S RIGHT!

PUHA (GASP)

THAT'S THE REASON WE'RE HERE.

WHAT IF I START FIGHTING THE WITCH WITHOUT KNOWING?

DON'T WORRY ABOUT IT.

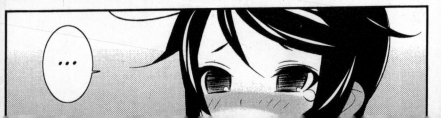

...

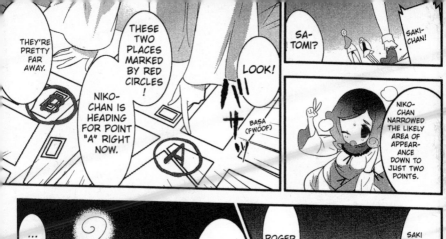

THEY'RE PRETTY FAR AWAY.

THESE TWO PLACES MARKED BY RED CIRCLES!

NIKO-CHAN IS HEADING FOR POINT "A" RIGHT NOW.

LOOK!

BASA (FWOOF)

SA-TOMI?

SAKI-CHAN!

NIKO-CHAN NARROWED THE LIKELY AREA OF APPEARANCE DOWN TO JUST TWO POINTS.

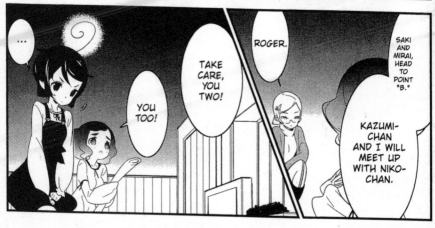

...

YOU TOO!

TAKE CARE, YOU TWO!

ROGER.

SAKI AND MIRAI, HEAD TO POINT "B."

KAZUMI-CHAN AND I WILL MEET UP WITH NIKO-CHAN.

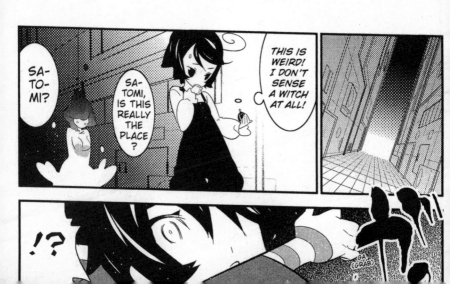

SA-TO-MI?

SA-TOMI, IS THIS REALLY THE PLACE?

THIS IS WEIRD! I DON'T SENSE A WITCH AT ALL!

!?

GA (GRAB)

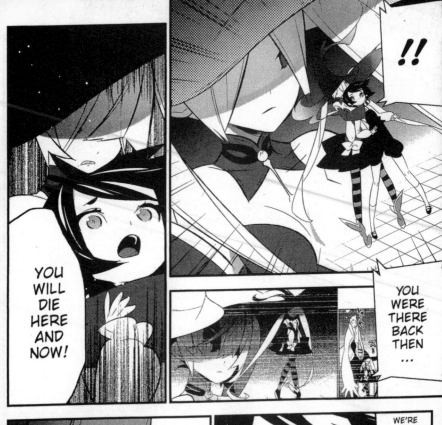

!!

YOU WILL DIE HERE AND NOW!

YOU WERE THERE BACK THEN...

WE'RE BOTH MAGICAL GIRLS! WHY DO WE HAVE TO KILL EACH OTHER?

YOU'RE ABOUT TO DIE.

WHY YOU NEED TO HEAR "WHY"?

YOU'RE THE ONE WHO STUFFED ME IN THE TRUNK, AREN'T YOU? WHY!?

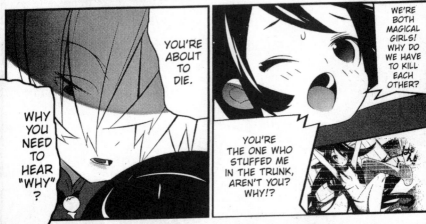

BA (WHOOSH)

!!

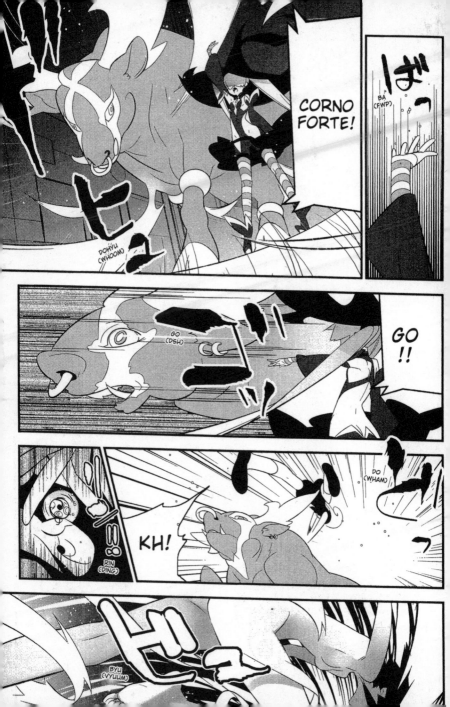

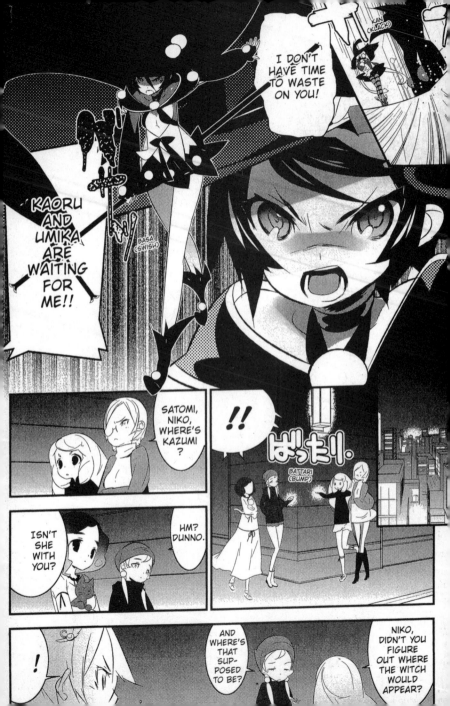

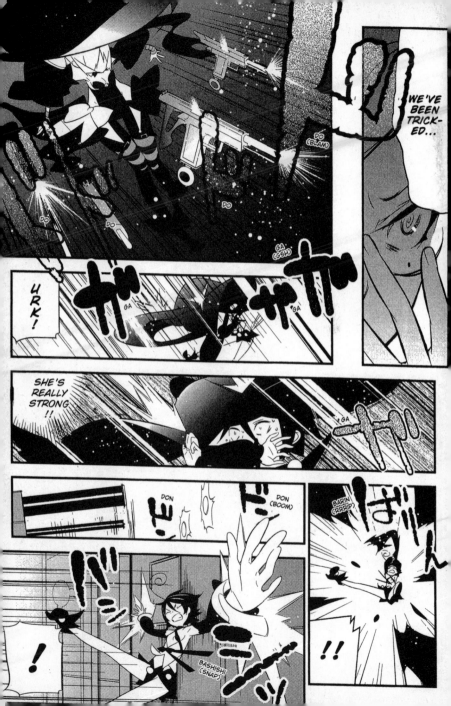

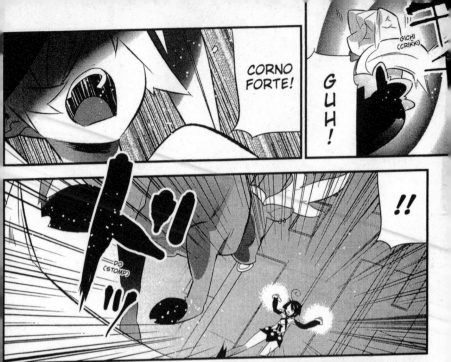

CORNO FORTE!

GUH!

GICHI
(CRIKKO)

!!

DO
(STOMP)

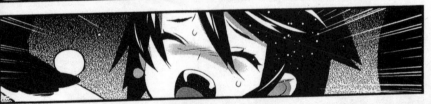

YOU GOT GUTS, TRYING TO PULL ONE OVER ON US.

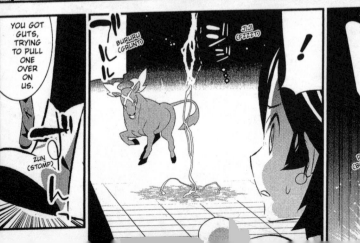

BURURU
(GRIND)

JIJI
(FIZZLE)

!

DO
(BOOM)

ZUN
(STOMP)

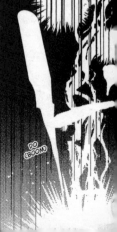

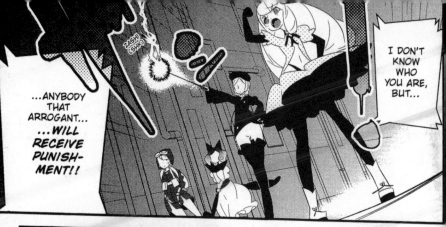

I DON'T KNOW WHO YOU ARE, BUT...

ZASH (SFX)

...ANYBODY THAT ARROGANT... ...WILL RECEIVE PUNISHMENT!!

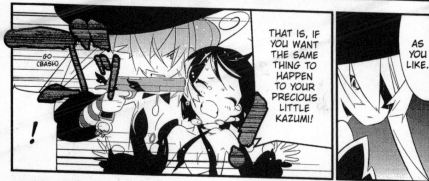

GO (BASH)

!

THAT IS, IF YOU WANT THE SAME THING TO HAPPEN TO YOUR PRECIOUS LITTLE KAZUMI!

AS YOU LIKE.

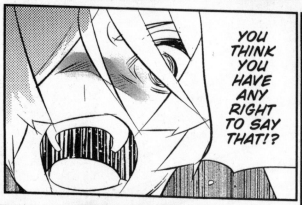

YOU THINK YOU HAVE ANY RIGHT TO SAY THAT!?

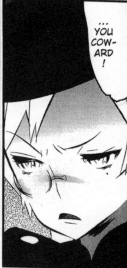

...YOU COWARD!

...

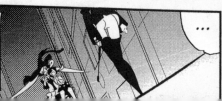

WELL? ARE YOU GOING TO ATTACK, OR AREN'T YOU!?

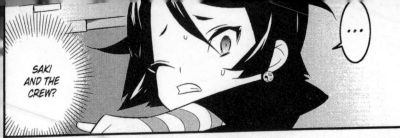

SAKI AND THE CREW?

...

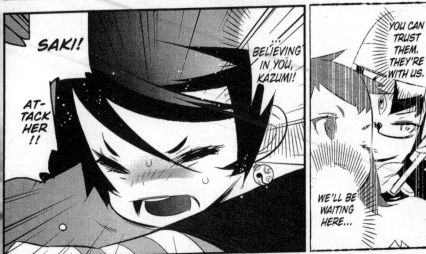

SAKI!

AT-TACK HER!!

...BELIEVING IN YOU, KAZUMI!!

YOU CAN TRUST THEM. THEY'RE WITH US.

WE'LL BE WAITING HERE...

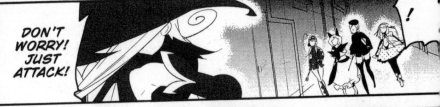

DON'T WORRY! JUST ATTACK!

!

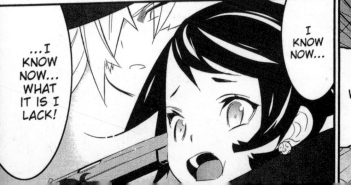

...I KNOW NOW... WHAT IT IS I LACK!

I KNOW NOW...

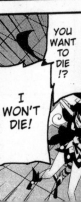

YOU WANT TO DIE!?

I WON'T DIE!

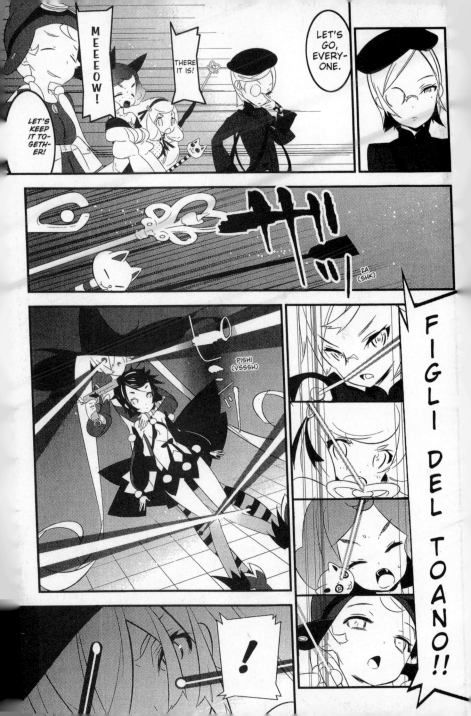

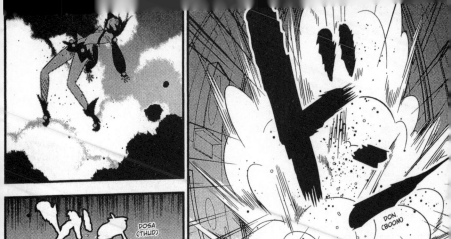

DOSA (THUD)

DON (BOOM)

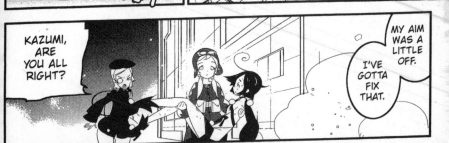

KAZUMI, ARE YOU ALL RIGHT?

MY AIM WAS A LITTLE OFF.

I'VE GOTTA FIX THAT.

KAZUMI-CHAN, YOU'RE WOUNDED—!

!

I'M FINE!

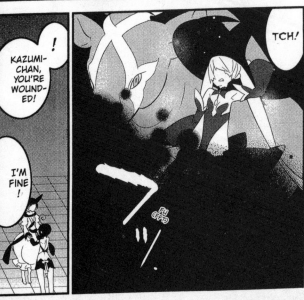

TCH!

FU GAD

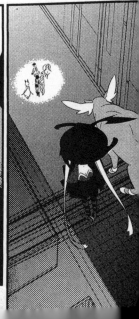

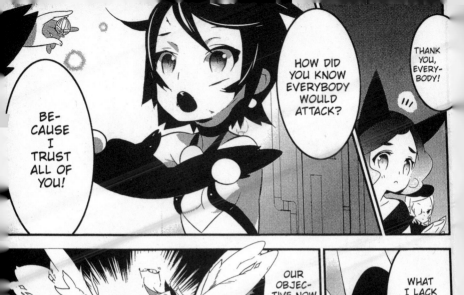

HOW DID YOU KNOW EVERYBODY WOULD ATTACK?

THANK YOU, EVERYBODY!

BE-CAUSE I TRUST ALL OF YOU!

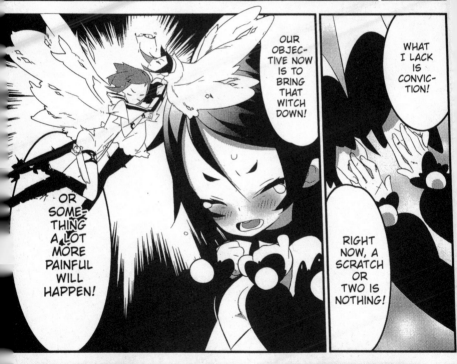

OUR OBJEC-TIVE NOW IS TO BRING THAT WITCH DOWN!

WHAT I LACK IS CONVIC-TION!

OR SOME-THING A LOT MORE PAINFUL WILL HAPPEN!

RIGHT NOW, A SCRATCH OR TWO IS NOTHING!

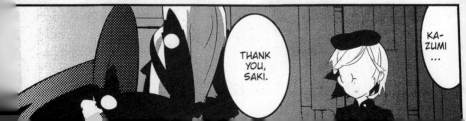

THANK YOU, SAKI.

KA-ZUMI...

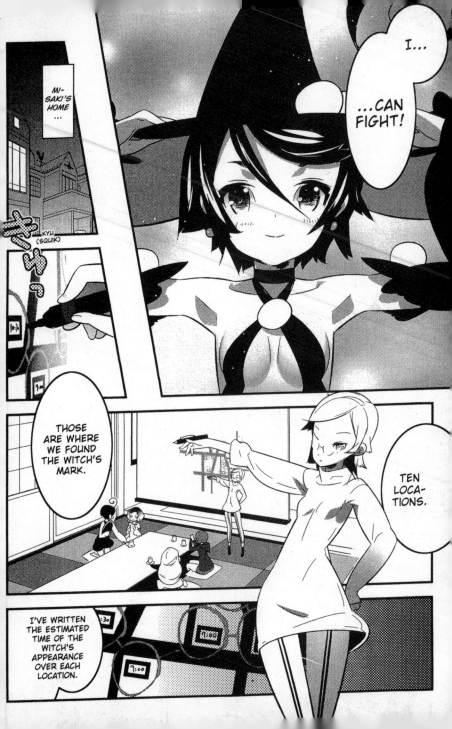

DUN- NO.

SO WHERE IS THE NEXT APPEAR- ANCE?

THE WITCH MOVES EVERY FORTY MINUTES.

WE DE- TERMINED A SCHEDULE FOR THE APPEAR- ANCES BASED ON THE STRENGTH OF THE MAGIC OF EACH MARK ...

... AND WE FOUND A PATTERN.

THE ONLY OTHER CLUE IS THIS MARK.

THEN IT DOESN'T MEAN ANY- THING!

I'VE SEEN IT SOME- WHERE ...

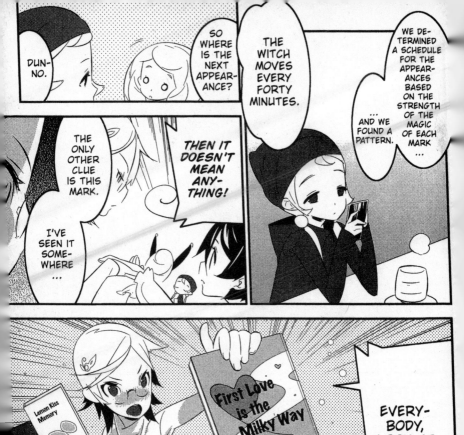

EVERY- BODY, LOOK AT THIS!!

Lemon Kiss Memory

Love

First Love is the Milky Way

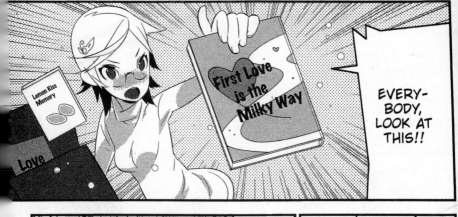

THIS MARK!

DON'T READ IT!! THAT ISN'T WHAT I'M TALKING ABOUT !!

FIRST LOVE IS THE MILKY WAY...

FIRST LOVE IS THE MILKY WAY...

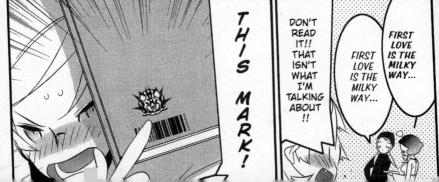

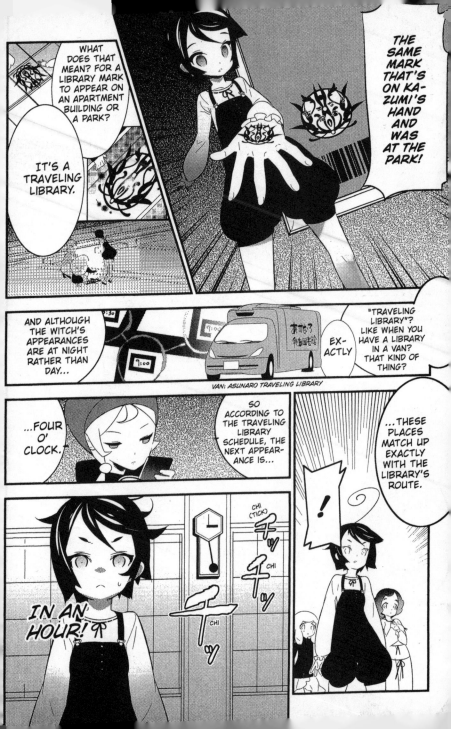

WHAT DOES THAT MEAN? FOR A LIBRARY MARK TO APPEAR ON AN APARTMENT BUILDING OR A PARK?

IT'S A TRAVELING LIBRARY.

THE SAME MARK THAT'S ON KAZUMI'S HAND AND WAS AT THE PARK!

AND ALTHOUGH THE WITCH'S APPEARANCES ARE AT NIGHT RATHER THAN DAY...

EXACTLY

"TRAVELING LIBRARY"? LIKE WHEN YOU HAVE A LIBRARY IN A VAN? THAT KIND OF THING?

VAN: ASUNARO TRAVELING LIBRARY

...FOUR O' CLOCK.

SO ACCORDING TO THE TRAVELING LIBRARY SCHEDULE, THE NEXT APPEARANCE IS...

...THESE PLACES MATCH UP EXACTLY WITH THE LIBRARY'S ROUTE.

CHI (TICK)

CHI

CHI

IN AN HOUR!

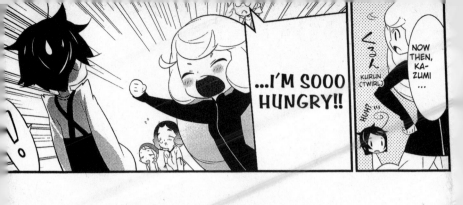
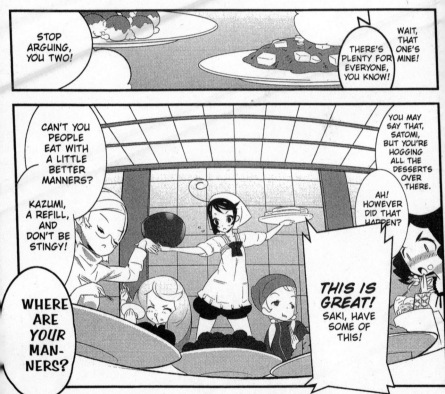
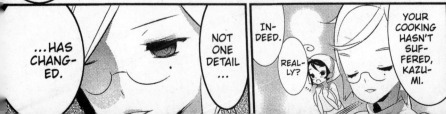

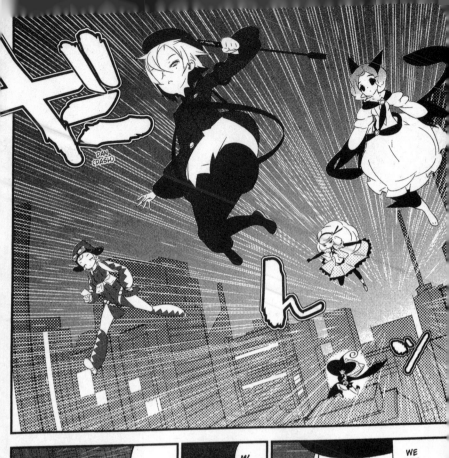

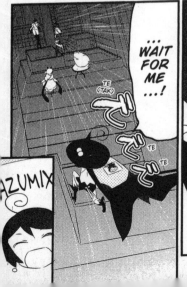

... WAIT FOR ME ...!

W...

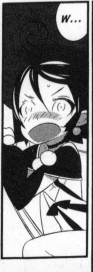

WE ARE NOW FORTIFIED WITH NUTRITION!

WE HAVE TO HURRY TO THE NEXT STOP!

YES, MA'AM!

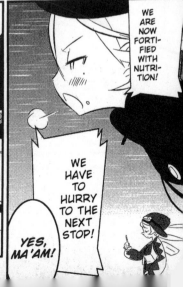

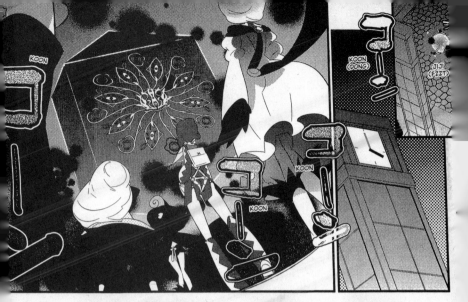

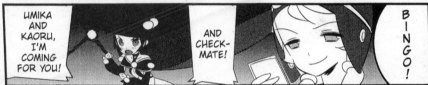

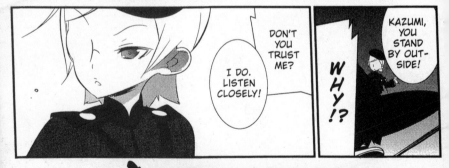

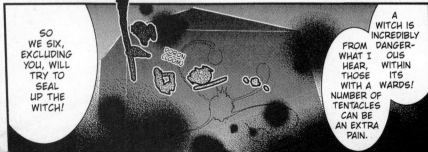

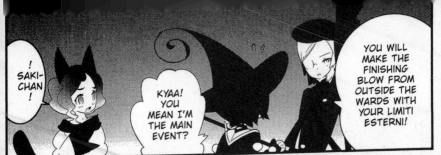

SAKI-CHAN!

KYAA! YOU MEAN I'M THE MAIN EVENT?

YOU WILL MAKE THE FINISHING BLOW FROM OUTSIDE THE WARDS WITH YOUR LIMITI ESTERNI!

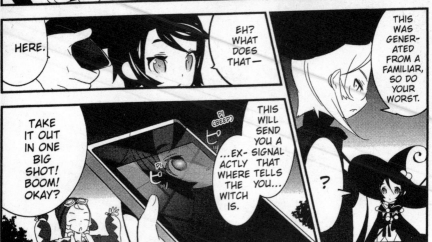

HERE.

EH? WHAT DOES THAT—

THIS WAS GENERATED FROM A FAMILIAR, SO DO YOUR WORST.

TAKE IT OUT IN ONE BIG SHOT! BOOM! OKAY?

THIS WILL SEND YOU A SIGNAL THAT TELLS YOU...

...EXACTLY WHERE THE WITCH IS.

PI (BEEP)

PI (BEEP)

?

WE TRUST IN YOU, KAZUMI.

GYU (SQUEEZE)

YEAH!

JUST LIKE YOU TRUSTED IN US.

OH, WAIT!

SO IS EVERYONE PREPARED?

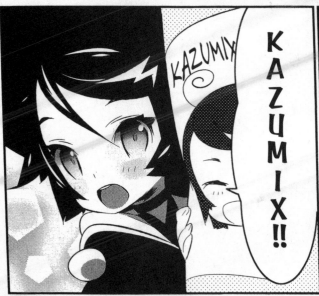

KAZUMI!

KAZUMI!!

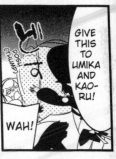

GIVE THIS TO UMIKA AND KAORU!

WAH!

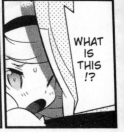

WHAT IS THIS!?

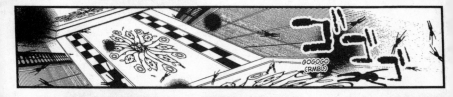

GOGOGO (RMBL)

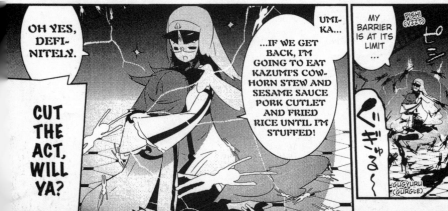

OH YES, DEFINITELY.

CUT THE ACT, WILL YA?

UMIKA...

...IF WE GET BACK, I'M GOING TO EAT KAZUMI'S COWHORN STEW AND SESAME SAUCE PORK CUTLET AND FRIED RICE UNTIL I'M STUFFED!

MY BARRIER IS AT ITS LIMIT...

PISHI (VLLIP)

GUGYURU (GURGLE)

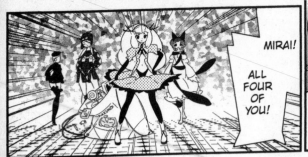

MIRAI!

ALL FOUR OF YOU!

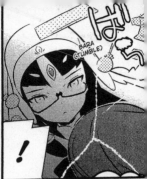

BARA (TUMBLE)

!

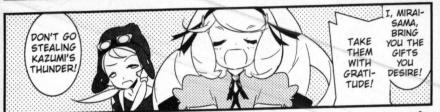

I, MIRAI-SAMA, BRING YOU THE GIFTS YOU DESIRE!

TAKE THEM WITH GRATITUDE!

DON'T GO STEALING KAZUMI'S THUNDER!

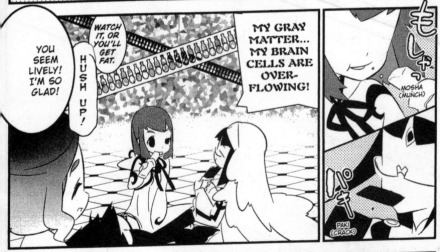

YOU SEEM LIVELY! I'M SO GLAD!

HUSH UP!

WATCH IT, OR YOU'LL GET FAT.

MY GRAY MATTER... MY BRAIN CELLS ARE OVER-FLOWING!

MOSHA (MUNCH)

PAKI (CRACK)

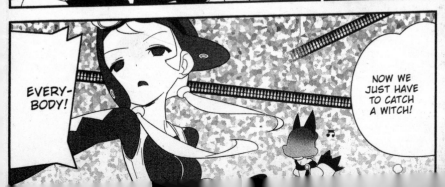

EVERY-BODY!

NOW WE JUST HAVE TO CATCH A WITCH!

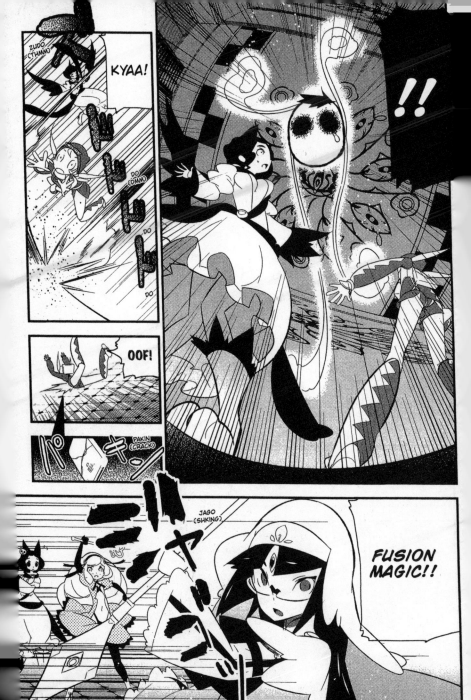

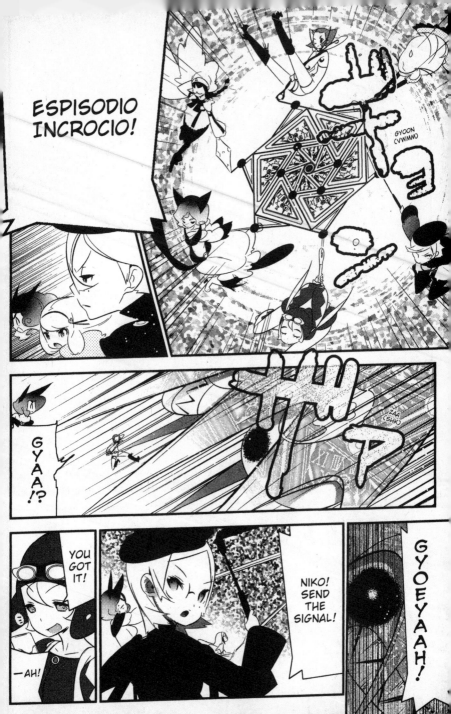

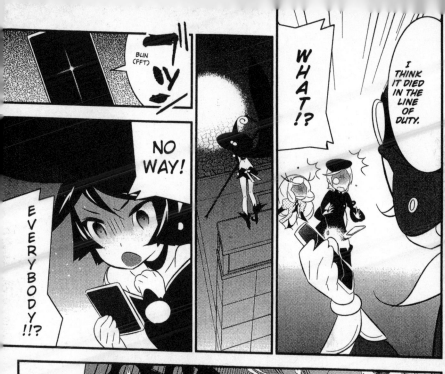
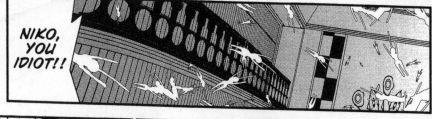
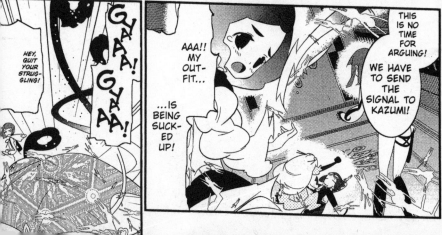

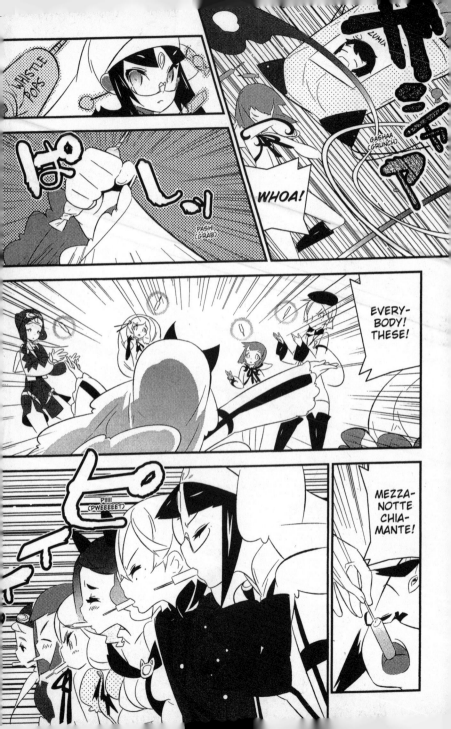

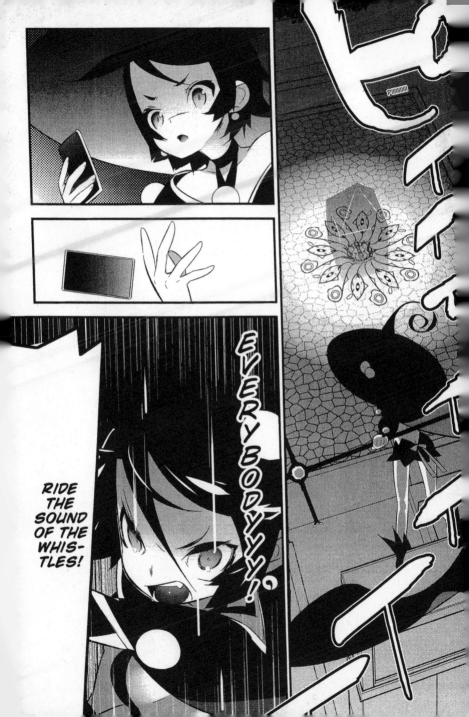

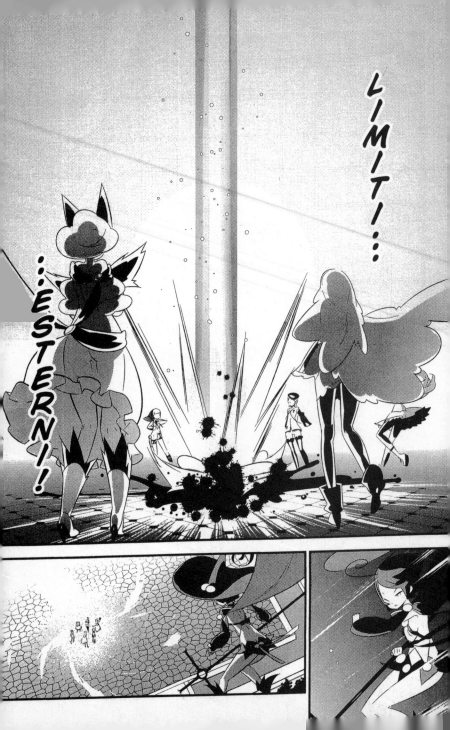

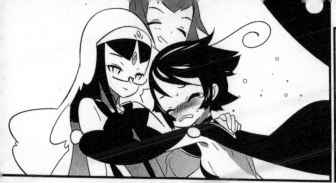

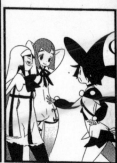

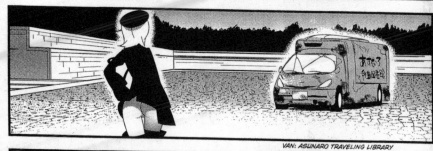

VAN: ASUNARO TRAVELING LIBRARY

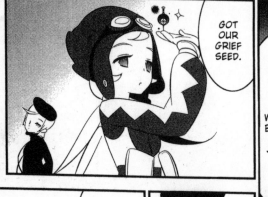

GOT OUR GRIEF SEED.

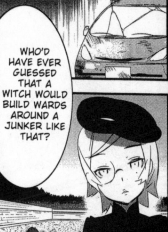

WHO'D HAVE EVER GUESSED THAT A WITCH WOULD BUILD WARDS AROUND A JUNKER LIKE THAT?

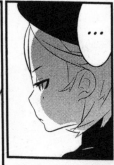

...

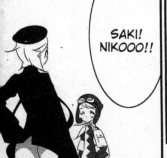

SAKI! NIKOOO!!

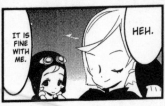

IT IS FINE WITH ME.

HEH.

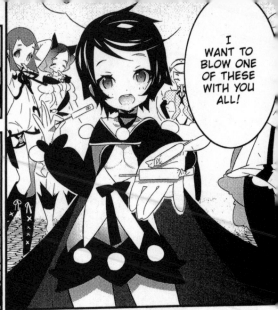

I WANT TO BLOW ONE OF THESE WITH YOU ALL!

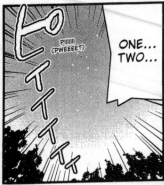

PIIIIIII! (PWEEEET)

ONE... TWO...

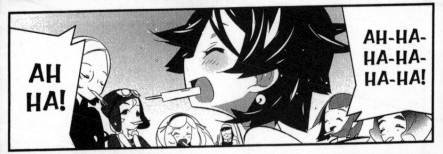

AH HA!

AH-HA-HA-HA-HA-HA!

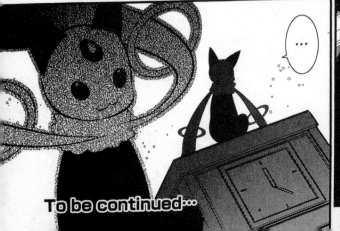

...

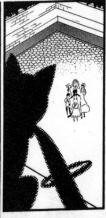

To be continued···

CHAPTER 3 WITCH: CALLSIGN "PROLOGUE"

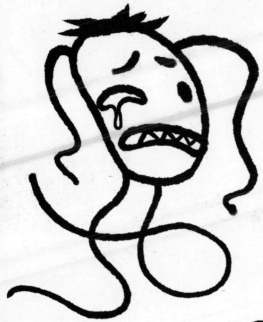

I TRIED TO MAKE
DESIGNS BASED ON
DRAWINGS KIDS MIGHT
DO IN A LIBRARY.
(TENSUGI)

A REJECTED PROLOGUE→
I GET THE FEELING NOW
THAT THIS ONE WOULD
HAVE BEEN A LITTLE
MORE APPROPRIATE.

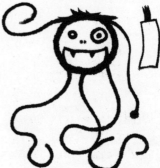

THE FAMILIARS↓
BOOKMARK PEOPLE.

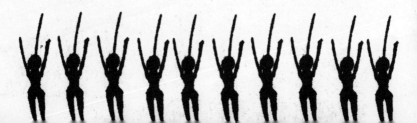

EVERYBODY'S ☆ MAGICA CLUB

With MASAKI HIRAMATSU

☆ Masaki Hiramatsu-sensei ☆
Art by: Fuyuno☆Magica-san

STORY WRITER MASAKI HIRAMATSU-SENSEI
ANSWERS THESE QUESTIONS AND THOSE QUESTIONS!

Q1 CIAO, HIRAMACCI! I DREW YOUR PORTRAIT TO BE AN EXACT LIKENESS, JUST AS YOU ORDERED!
(FUYUNO☆MAGICA-SAN)

HIRAMACCHI: CIAO! FUYUNO☆MAGICA-SAN IS THE DAUGHTER OF A COWORKER OF MINE, M-SAN. SHE'S CURRENTLY IN HER THIRD YEAR OF MIDDLE SCHOOL!! I NEVER GET ANY FAN MAIL, SO I HAD HER DRAW SOMETHING FOR ME. IT LOOKS JUST LIKE ME! I LOVE IT! OF COURSE, I WAS BORN WITH THIS FACE AND HAVE NEVER HAD A GIRL CONFESS HER LOVE TO ME...

Q2 CIAO, HIRAMACCI! THIS IS A SPIN-OFF OF "MADOKA," BUT THE DETAILS OF THE SETTING SEEM A BIT DIFFERENT?
(MANGA☆MAGICA-SAN)

HIRAMACCHI: CIAO! THAT'S ODD... I READ ALL OF THE SCRIPTS BEFORE I STARTED WRITING KAZUMI, AND WE CLEARED IT WITH OUR SUPERVISORS... IT MATCHES! I'M SURE IT MATCHES!

Q3 CIAO, HIRAMACCI! WHERE'S KYUBEY?
(TIME☆MAGICA-SAN)

HIRAMACCHI: CIAO...HUH? WHAT IS THIS "KYUBEY" AGAIN...?
EDITOR N: HEY...WAIT...DON'T GO GIVING AWAY SPOILERS, PLEASE...

Q6 HIRAMATSU-SAN! WHEN CAN I EXPECT THE NEXT SCRIPT?
(N☆MAGICA-SAN)

HIRAMACCHI: UM...THE SCRIPT... UH...N-SAN, COULD WE HAVE A MEETING? AT THE SAME OLD MEETING PLACE? AND SO WE'RE EAGERLY AWAITING YOUR QUESTIONS AND FAN ART. SO WE'LL SEE YOU IN VOLUME TWO! ONE, TWO, THREE...BUH-BYYYE!

Q4 CIAO, HIRAMACCI! WHAT DOES THE SUBTITLE, "THE INNOCENT MALICE" MEAN?
(KIRARA☆MAGICA-SAN)

HIRAMACCHI: MY DICTIONARY DEFINES THE WORDS AS "NAÏVE EVIL INTENT."

Q5 CIAO, HIRAMACCI! HOW LONG DO YOU INTEND TO KEEP NAMING CHAPTER TITLES AFTER FOOD?
(FORWARD☆MAGICA-SAN)

HIRAMACCHI: I'VE GOT NO BETTER IDEAS, AND I'M HEARING SOME GOOD FOOD SUGGESTIONS, SO...

WE'D LIKE YOUR PSEUDONYM FOR THIS QUESTION CORNER TO BE XXX☆MAGICA, OKAY? YOU CAN MAKE IT WHATEVER YOU WANT, AS LONG AS IT'S THREE SYLLABLES!

THIS IS TENSUGI'S VERY FIRST MANGA VOLUME.
THANK YOU, EDITOR N-SAMA, HOUBUNSHA'S FORWARD EDITORIAL
DEPARTMENT, AND EVERYONE OF THE MAGICA COMMITTEE...

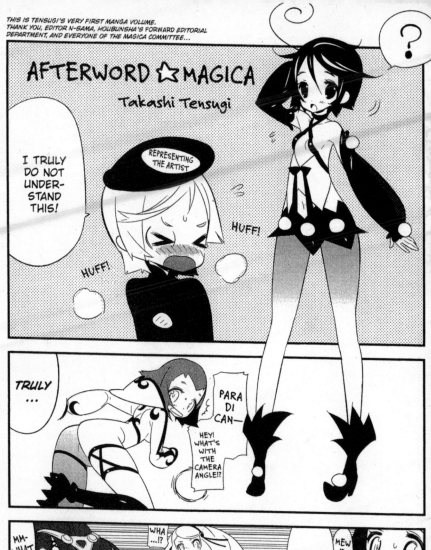

AFTERWORD ☆ MAGICA

Takashi Tensugi

I TRULY DO NOT UNDERSTAND THIS!

REPRESENTING THE ARTIST

HUFF!

HUFF!

?

TRULY ...

PARA DI CAN—

HEY! WHAT'S WITH THE CAMERA ANGLE!?

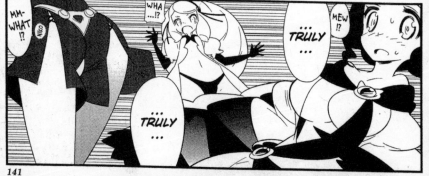

MM— WHAT !?

WHA ...!?

... TRULY ...

MEW !?

... TRULY ...

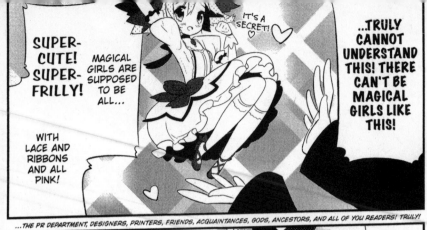

SUPER-CUTE! SUPER-FRILLY!

MAGICAL GIRLS ARE SUPPOSED TO BE ALL...

IT'S A SECRET!

...TRULY CANNOT UNDERSTAND THIS! THERE CAN'T BE MAGICAL GIRLS LIKE THIS!

WITH LACE AND RIBBONS AND ALL PINK!

...THE PR DEPARTMENT, DESIGNERS, PRINTERS, FRIENDS, ACQUAINTANCES, GODS, ANCESTORS, AND ALL OF YOU READERS! TRULY!

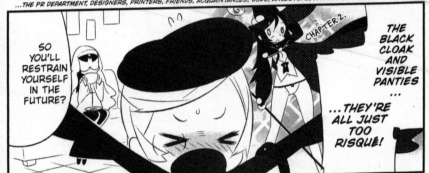

SO YOU'LL RESTRAIN YOURSELF IN THE FUTURE?

CHAPTER 2.

THE BLACK CLOAK AND VISIBLE PANTIES...

...THEY'RE ALL JUST TOO RISQUÉ!

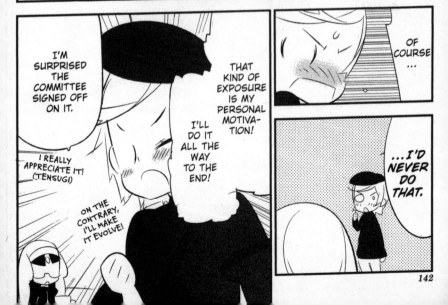

I'M SURPRISED THE COMMITTEE SIGNED OFF ON IT.

THAT KIND OF EXPOSURE IS MY PERSONAL MOTIVATION!

I'LL DO IT ALL THE WAY TO THE END!

I REALLY APPRECIATE IT! (TENSUGI)

ON THE CONTRARY, I'LL MAKE IT EVOLVE!

OF COURSE...

...I'D NEVER DO THAT.

142

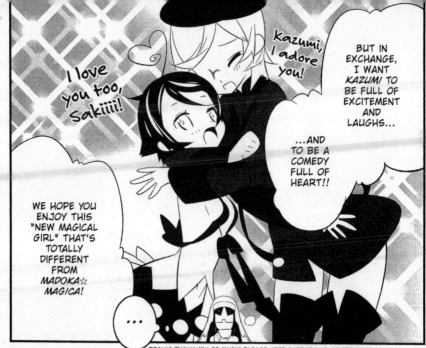

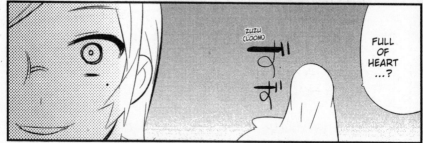

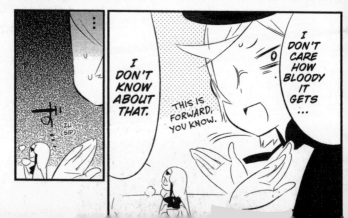

PUELLA MAGI
KAZUMI ★ MAGICA
The innocent malice

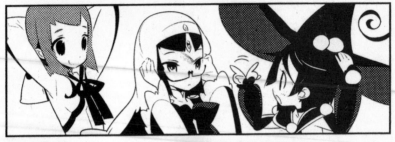

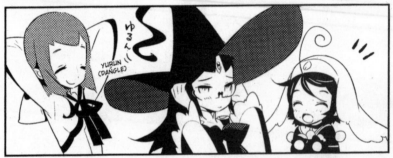

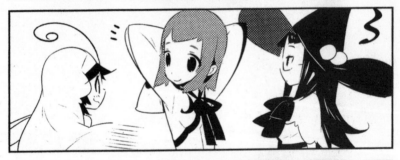

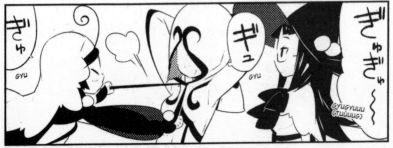

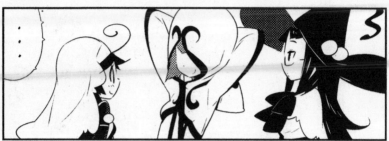

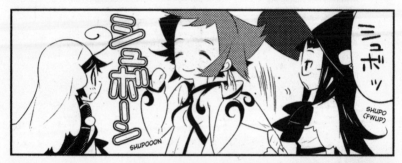

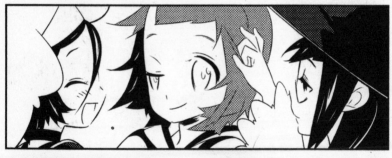

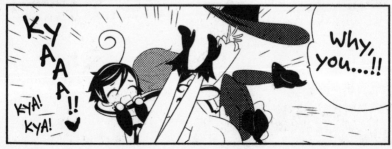

PUELLA MAGI
KAZUMI☆MAGICA
~The innocent malice~ ❶

MAGICA QUARTET
MASAKI HIRAMATSU
TAKASHI TENSUGI

Translation: William Flanagan • Lettering: Carl Vanstiphout

MAHO SHOJO KAZUMI ☆ MAGICA ~The innocent malice~ vol. 1
© 2011 Magica Quartet / Aniplex, Madoka Partners, MBS. All rights reserved. First published in Japan in 2011 by HOUBUNSHA CO., LTD, Tokyo. English translation rights in United States, Canada, and United Kingdom arranged with HOUBUNSHA CO., LTD. through Tuttle-Mori Agency, Inc., Tokyo.

Translation © 2013 by Hachette Book Group, Inc.

Yen Press
Hachette Book Group
1290 Avenue of the Americas, New York, NY 10104

www.HachetteBookGroup.com
www.YenPress.com

Yen Press is an imprint of Hachette Book Group, Inc. The Yen Press name and logo are trademarks of Hachette Book Group, Inc.

First Yen Press Edition: June 2013

ISBN: 978-0-316-25096-2

10 9 8 7 6 5 4 3 2

BVG

Printed in the United States of America